Karson's Journey

Reflections of a Grieving Mother

Lou Bickerstaff

Kevin Bickerstaff

214·675·0711

ISBN 978-1-64114-860-3 (paperback)
ISBN 978-1-64114-861-0 (digital)

Christian Faith Publishing, Inc.
832 Park Avenue
Meadville, PA 16335
www.christianfaithpublishing.com

Printed in the United States of America

In memory of Karson Grace Bickerstaff,
thank you for giving me the priceless gift
of being a mom for the very first time.
August 7, 2003 to August 19, 2003.

Dedicated to her dad,
my friend, my soul mate, my love
forever and a day.

In honor of Jesus Christ,
the giver of life and the keeper of my soul.

Special thanks
to my Aunt Marjorie, for offering her expertise in editing.
Your honesty and encouragement have given me
the courage to let others read this book.
To my dad, Bill Koehn, for volunteering your time and experience.
Your words always strike near to my heart.

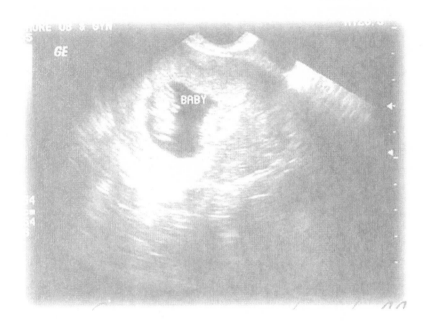

*For you created my inmost being; you knit
me together in my mother's womb.
I will praise you because I am fearfully and wonderfully made;
and your works are wonderful, I know them full well. My
frame was not hidden from you when I was made in the secret
place. When I was woven together in the depths of the earth,
your eyes saw my unformed body. All the days ordained for me
were written in your book before one of them came to be.*

—Psalm 139:13–16

Prologue

As I start to write this memorial about my daughter, Karson Grace, it has been nearly two weeks since her passing. In those two weeks, I have felt a pain unlike any other. It is a deep gut-wrenching anguish that floods my heart and soul over and over. Not only does it hurt emotionally, it literally takes on a physical form at times. There are those rare moments when I think I'm going to be okay—those first few minutes when I wake up in the morning and it feels like just another day. Then it hits me. No, more like overwhelms me, and the wave of emotions envelope me all over again.

I suspect, and am told by others who have experience similar losses, that these feelings will continue for months, maybe even years, before the pain merely diminishes to a dull ache. So the best and only way that I know to express how I am feeling, and possibly start the healing process in my life, is to write about my experience and the incredible life of our precious baby girl. I want to share it with whoever will listen. I am so proud to be her mom, and even though I don't have my daughter here in the flesh, it thrills me to show her off and to share her story with you.

So much has happened from the time that I discovered I was pregnant to her birth and eventually her death. I'm not sure it can even all be put into words. Just in case my attempt to describe the last ten months fails, please take time to look at the pictures incorporated throughout this book. Whoever it was that said a picture is worth a thousand words knew what he was talking about. The joy, pain, and awe of Karson is written on each face, and if you look close enough, they tell a story all their own.

In His Likeness

I found out I was pregnant for the third time in two years in December of 2002. My husband, Kevin, and I were both excited and a little leery as we had lost the last two babies in miscarriages. I insisted that we wait to tell everyone until I was through the first trimester. At times, it was hard to keep the news from our family and friends, but the fear of another failed pregnancy kept us both on guard.

Finally, in February, after an ultrasound confirmed the baby was growing and the heartbeat was audibly detected, we started to let our family and friends in on the good news. I hadn't made it past the first ten weeks with the others, so when we passed the twelve-week mark and could visibly see growth taking place, I started to believe this time might actually be different. My prayers, however, were still said with some lingering doubt. "Please, dear God, let me have this baby. I promise to raise him or her in your image and give everything I have to this child you have created for me. More than anything, I want to be a mom. Please let me have this baby."

Since I had trouble with the last two pregnancies, my doctor, John Becker, scheduled me for prenatal checkups every two weeks. Not only did it help him evaluate how things were going, but it also helped ease my fears about something going wrong. With each appointment, the heartbeat became stronger and clearer, and the ultrasounds continued to show steady growth. As I approached the halfway point, I started to feel the baby kick, and I really began to get excited. I couldn't wait for my twenty-week appointment. Normally, this is the one where expectant parents find out the sex of their baby. However, my husband I had decided we wanted it to be a surprise, so I was just going to videotape the ultrasound and not let them point out any gender areas to me. Even before we found out I was pregnant, Kevin was forthright about wanting a boy, but I knew that when it came down to it, it wouldn't matter to either of us as long as the child was healthy.

My twenty-week appointment was on a Friday. Everything went great as far as I was concerned; however, when Dr. Becker left a message for me at work fours days later, I knew something was wrong, t herefore beginning the longest five months of our lives.

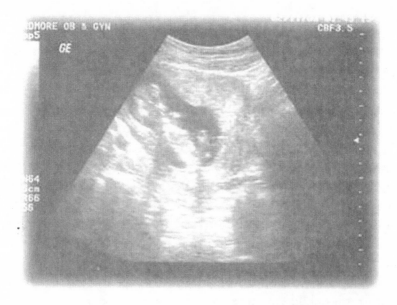

From Bad to Worse

Dr. Becker explained that the ultrasound tech believed, and he concurred after looking at the photos, that the baby's heart was on the wrong side, a disorder called dextrocardia. Although a relatively known term in the medical field, it was not something that either Kevin or I had heard about. Needless to say, we were beside ourselves with worry. As Dr. Becker made an appointment with a fetal specialist for us the next day, I frantically searched the Internet for information about the disorder. I was looking for whatever I could find—that one report that would tell me our baby could still live even if what they suspected was true. Amazingly, that is what I found, and although my anxiety level was greatly accelerated, I still held hope that our baby would be okay. Surely God wouldn't bring us this far only to let us down again. The next day, Kevin and I made our way to Oklahoma City to OU Medical Center where we had an appointment with Dr. John Stanley.

My husband had never seen an ultrasound before. He sat in amazement as Dr. Stanley looked at every part of our unborn child. He measured the head, the stomach and limbs, he looked at the flow of the blood in and out of the heart, and he confirmed for us the sex of our baby. We changed our minds about finding out on the way to the doctor's office that day. We figured we had already had enough surprises, and if there was something wrong with our baby, somehow knowing if it was a boy or girl and being able to give him or her a name suddenly became important to us. It didn't have anything to do with how the nursery would be decorated or the shower gifts. We just wanted every opportunity to bond with our baby and to know him or her inside and out, even before the birth.

We found out we were having a girl. Oh, believe me, Kevin had the doctor check a second time just to be sure, but like I said, it didn't really matter. As vocal as Kevin had been about wanting a boy, our little girl quickly had her mom and dad wrapped around her little finger. That day, Karson Grace became part of our family forever. We both knew we could never go back; this was a journey we had to take whether we wanted to or not.

Journal Entry from 4-9-03

We didn't get very good news about our baby girl today. Your heart (they think) is in the center of your body, and there appears to be a hole in the bottom chamber and possibly one in the top as well. It could be fixed with surgery after you are born. We are going to a pediatric cardiologist next week to find out more. The doctor is also concerned that you may have Down syndrome. This is a very hard thing for your mommy and daddy because we want you to have the fullest life possible, and this is just not something we were expecting. It's okay though, no matter what, we love you and cherish your life. You are a gift from God and perfect in our eyes. We believe God will give us the child that he created for us, so whether you have heart problems, Down syndrome, or something else altogether, you will always be our baby girl—our Karson Grace.

Email to Friends and Family on 4-15-03

Dearest friends and family,

I just wanted to send all of you a quick note of thanks. Kevin and I really appreciate all the prayers and words of kind encouragement. It means the world to us. As I sit here typing this, our baby girl is kicking away. It's hard for me to believe she isn't completely healthy. We went in for our regular checkup today, and her heartbeat was strong, and she continues to grow. A few days before we found out that there could be problems with our baby, I heard a new song on the radio. Then as I was driving home the day the doctor told us we needed to see a specialist, I heard it again. I am claiming the song for us. It has such powerful words of faith in it, and I truly believe that God gave me that song to offer my heart some peace in a time of such uncertainty. I thought I would share the words with you so that you too can believe them and claim them for our baby.

There lived a man and a women
In a town called Shunem

They made home for Elisha
And found favor in his eyes
So God sent them a miracle

14

KARSON'S JOURNEY

The only thing they longed for
Within the year they would hold a son
As Elisha prophesied

One day they ran from the field
Brought the child to his mother
She held his head there on her knee
Until he died at noon that day
She didn't tell anyone
She ran straight to the man of God
And if anybody asked her
She replied while on her way
It is well, it is well

There is peace in my despair
Knowing God has heard my prayer
And I will cling to the promise that He brings
Even death can have no sting
No power in hell
In His presence I will dwell
Where it is well

Elisha stood by the bedside
Where she laid the boy when he died
He prayed a prayer upon him
And he breathed new life again
Friend, God doesn't ever change
If you'll have that woman's faith
He'll send you a miracle
And until then you can say

It is well, it is well
There is peace in my despair
Knowing God has heard my prayer
And I will cling to the promise that He brings
Even death can have no sting

No power in hell
In his presence I will dwell
For it is well[1]

We love you all. Please keep us in your prayers tomorrow as we go to see the pediatric cardiologist. We'll let you know how it goes.

Kevin, Lou, and Karson Grace

The next day, Karson's Granny Nene (Kevin's mom) went with me to my appointment with the pediatric cardiologist, Dr. Kent Ward. He did another ultrasound and, within a few minutes, confirmed Dr. Stanley's suspicions about the two holes in her heart. He also said there was an aortic valve that wasn't functioning properly. The good news, huge news to me at the time, was that he didn't see anything that couldn't be repaired after she was born. He couldn't give us a time frame in which surgery would have to be done, but he thought by the time she was two years old, she would have a fully functional heart and be running and playing like all the other kids.

We had also decided to have an amniocentesis done that day so that we could know better if the suspicion of Down syndrome was valid. This in itself was an experience I will never forget. Although Dr. Stanley finally got what he needed, Karson showed her ornery personality that day. She was in perfect position when he went in with the needle to get the fluid for the amnio, but the minute that needle invaded her space, she stuck her little rear end right up in the way. The doctor and nurse pushed every which way on my stomach to get her to move, but she wouldn't budge. Dr. Stanley even got frustrated enough to call her a little toot. I don't think he thought she was very funny, but I did, and her dad was sure proud when I told him about it. There was no doubt she was his little girl.

---

[1] "It is Well (Elisha's Song)" by Rebecca Isaacs Bowman and Sonya Isaacs @ copyright R.I. Bowman Music/BMI/Miss Surrett Music/BMI (both admin by ICG). All rights reserved. Used by permission.

I left the doctor feeling good that day. No, it wasn't the best news we could've received, but at least they didn't tell me she was going to die, and to me that was all I needed to know.

Both Kevin and I were at work the next day, feeling as if some of our burden had been lifted. I was in a meeting that afternoon when one of the ladies I work with, Theresa Matthews, paged me and asked me to come back to my office right away. She didn't tell me why, and I didn't bother to ask; I just thought it was business related. When I walked in the office, Dr. Becker was there. Even then, it didn't sink in that he was there with more bad news. Silly one that I am, I just thought he had stopped by to say hi. He didn't beat around the bush; he just gently told me that Dr. Stanley had called with the preliminary results from the amnio, and there was evidence that Karson had a genetic disorder involving the thirteenth chromosome—trisomy 13.

Journal Entry from 4-17-03

Today we got the worst news we could possibly ever get. The doctor called with the preliminary results from the amnio. It shows you have trisomy 13. If that is true, they don't expect you to live more than a few days. Your dad and I want you to know that we will never give up on you— we pray that God will choose to bring a miracle into our lives and let you live a healthy life with us for many years. But no matter what happens, you will always be our baby girl—Karson Grace—and we will love you forever. There are prayers being lifted up all over the United States for you. God is in control, and he loves you even more than we do, and he will take care of all of us through this.

The only reason I even knew what trisomy 13 meant was because when Dr. Stanley had told us he thought she might have Down syndrome, he also told us about two terminal genetic disorders, trisomy 13 and 18. He said there was a 1 percent chance—one in five thousand chance—that she would have either of them and that the odds for Down's was much greater, so we both took for granted there was no way she could have trisomy 13 or 18.

I don't know how to describe my feelings when I heard the news. I went numb. I remember telling Dr. Becker and my two friends that were there that I didn't know what to do now. I think if it had been an option, I would've sat in the same chair, in the same spot, for the rest of the day and not moved for fear that if I did, what they were saying would really be true. By staying motionless, somehow it would stop all the bad from happening. Time would just stand still.

I don't remember the exact date that I first felt Karson kick me, but I remember her kicking me that day. It was my wakeup call. Her telling me that she was still there; even though they had just given her a death sentence, she was alive and kicking right now. In her own way, it was just the beginning to her watching over her mom, a sign to me that she was—and would be—okay no matter what happened.

After a brief conversation with Dr. Stanley on the phone, Trish Long, one of my dearest friends and stand-in mom, got Kevin on the phone. I kept telling her not to call him. I knew he was just getting ready to leave on a flight, and I didn't want to tell him the news right before he left when there was nothing he could do. She called him anyway. When she handed me the phone, I said hi, and that's when I lost it. We didn't say a word for a minute or two; we just cried as if there wasn't a phone and thousands of miles between us.

I actually ended up driving to Oklahoma City that night to meet Kevin when he came in instead of having him drive all the way home, as he had to leave again on another trip the next day. I will never forget the look of emotional pain on his face when I walked into that hotel room. It was one I pray I never see again. It was a reflection of all that I was feeling, and it broke my heart into a thousand pieces. I don't remember our words to each other; we just hung on to each other for dear life, with Karson right there in the middle of us kicking away.

Kevin's Journal Entry from 4-17-03

Karson Grace Bickerstaff, Dad loves you, Mom loves you. May God hold you in his arms until I get there. I love you, little girl. I just hope someway God lets you know how much Mom and Dad love you.

A Strong Foundation

Kevin and I have been married for three and a half years. We have what I would consider a great marriage and a close relationship. But that day on the phone, something more than our crying together took place. I felt a need to cling to my husband like never before. He was the only other person that could possibly understand how I was feeling, the only other one who knew the panic welling up inside of me. It is true that we react and even express our pain in different ways, but it is still the same intimate pain.

As Kevin started back to Oklahoma that afternoon, we both knew we would only have one night together before he went back to work the next day. In the minds of some, it might have been cruel for him to leave me and go back to work, but to me it wasn't. His way of dealing with the hurt and fear was to stay busy. Mine is to retreat from everyone for a few days until I have processed what I am experiencing. We both knew how important it was to let each other grieve in the way that worked best for us.

Looking back, I think it is all part of the big picture. Believe me, I still don't see the whole picture. I have a lot of questions for God someday, but little by little, he is allowing me glimpses as to what it looks like. Your picture may not look the same, but this is how I see mine. We are all on a journey through life. Because of free will, we are allowed to make our own decisions, whether they are part of God's perfect plan for us or not. Both Kevin and I made some of those decisions years ago. They eventually led us to each other. For both of us, one of those decisions was also a recommitment to Jesus Christ early on in our relationship. At that time, we allowed him to take over, and he began to lead us down the path we are currently on. As Corrie Ten

Boone once said, "Every experience God gives us, every person he puts in our life is perfect preparation for the future that only he can see." He began to prepare us for this journey at this time in our lives.

I praise God for that preparation and for our relationship with each other. Kevin doesn't believe it to this day, but he has been my anchor from the moment we started getting bad news. Without him, I would've sank into depression. He kept me grounded in life and didn't allow me to resort into a mountain of self-pity. He'd let me cry, and then in his own unique way, he'd pick me up, dust me off, and send me back into the game. He is exactly the person I needed beside me—my soul mate through good and bad.

Email to Friends and Family on 4-19-03

As many of you have probably noticed, I am not very good at talking to anyone when we get bad news. As of Thursday, I haven't communicated with many of you at all. I hope you don't think I am being rude or that your thoughts and words of encouragement are not important to me. They are in fact, at times, my only lifeline. I just tend to go into a shell, and it is much easier for me if I can have some space to get my heart and mind to a place that I can talk about the things that are going on without completely breaking down each time. I know all of you would understand that kind of breakdown, but for me, it is just easier to do in private or with Kevin (and thankfully he lets me vent however I need to at the time). Although I am not always up to speaking the words, I do want to share my feelings with you and let you know where I am at with the news about Karson. First, I want to say that in no way are Kevin and I giving up on our daughter; she has fought to stay with us this long, and until God says otherwise, we will fight to keep her with us whether that is for a few hours, days, months or years.

In my heart, I am praying for a miracle of total and complete healing for Karson. I mean that from the bottom of my heart, and I know God has heard my prayer. Unfortunately, I don't know in which form that miracle will come. I hope it is his will for her to be healed in the flesh and that she can have many healthy, active, and precious years here on earth with us. However, I know there is an even far greater blessing for her if God chooses to take her home to be with him. Part of me is so angry with God for doing this to me, but as Kevin said to me the day we got the news, "This is no longer about you and me, it is about Karson and what is best for her." So as a mother that has yet to hold her child, I am giving her back to God for his complete love and protection.

Some good friends of mine that I work with gave me a book of prayers for healing and strength. My prayers continue without ceasing, but this is the special prayer I have for today: "Heavenly Father, I place myself in your hands, confident that you will be my strength and guide. I do not pray to you for health or sickness, neither life nor death, but rather that I be made strong in the grace and love of you. May your name be praised as I lift up my heart to you, my Savior. You know my needs, so I confidently place myself (and Karson) totally in your hands. Guide and bless me always. Lord, I am yours and yours I wish to be. Thy will be done. Amen."

I love you and will be in touch again soon.

Knowing Versus Not Knowing

I've often wondered if I had this to do all over again if I would want to know ahead of time what we were facing with our child. I see pros and cons both ways. The knowledge meant that for five months, we had to just wait and see what was going to happen. It made it hard to enjoy being pregnant. Do I decorate the nursery or not? Have a baby shower or not? Then there is the added fear of knowing the strong possibility that she may die before she is ever born. Every time I didn't feel her move for more than an hour or so, I would panic. There were nights I would wake up to go to the bathroom, and during the time I was up, she wouldn't move, so I would have to get her to make some kind of movement before I could comfortably go back to sleep. Some nights she would at least make a small move fairly quickly, but other nights it would take what seemed like hours before she would let me know she was okay. I would lie there tossing and turning, tapping and pressing, begging her to just kick me. Finally, she would move, and I could go back to sleep. It was at these moments I think it would've been easier not to have known her diagnosis.

On the other hand, it gave us time to prepare ourselves for the worst-case scenario. I can't imagine thinking I was having a healthy baby and, when she is born, losing her. That tragic shock has to be unbearable. The way it was we went through the shock and then tried to deal with it for five months. For me, that meant finding out as much information as I could about the disease and talking to doctors and nurses about how things might go at delivery. I even spent half a day at Mercy meeting the nurses in charge of the birthplace (Allison Quiroz) and the Neonatal Intensive Care Unit (NICU) (Michele McEver). I also met with the doctor that would take care of Karson (Dr. Rajkumar Reddy). It helped me get as prepared as I possibly could, and it meant something to me to know some of the people that would be taking care of us before we actually got there at the time of delivery.

Knowing also allowed us the chance to turn to God in prayer. Not that we weren't praying before we found out, but being faced with the death of your child makes the conversations with God a little bit more intense. It gave us the opportunity to lean on him more than we ever had before, as well as those family and friends around us.

My husband had many of the same feelings as I did, but he also had some additional ones to deal with. I think it was harder on him knowing ahead of time. Most men would probably feel much the same way as he did presented with the same situation because of a God-given characteristic to be the leader and the protector of the family. From the minute we found out something was wrong, he started searching for a way to fix it. The fact that he couldn't was extremely hard for him to deal with. He felt like he was letting his family down; he wasn't of course, but the feelings were very valid ones. He had a hard time letting himself get too attached to Karson. He did despite himself, but there was a constant battle in his heart not to get too consumed by her. He describes those five months as being on a roller coaster, and you can't get off. Every time you think the ride is coming to an end, it starts up all over again, taking you up and down, up and down.

I think it depends on the kind of person you are that really leads to the answer. For me, even with every bad doctor's report, I still chose to believe that my baby could be okay. If God wanted to heal her, he could. I believed a miracle could happen—she was already beating the odds, and if she was strong enough to fight for her life, I certainly wasn't going to be the one to give up on her. So I continued on the best I could as if everything was okay. I ate well, and I tried not to get to overworked or stressed out. Kevin and I read and sang to her. We talked to her, and we prayed for her without ceasing. In my mind, knowing what challenges lay ahead was a blessing. It gave me the opportunity to turn to God in my time of need, and it strengthened my faith.

Leaning on God

So many scriptures and songs seemed to speak right to me during this time. It's amazing the different ways God finds to talk to us in our time of need. Some of my favorites were the following:

> As you do not know the path of the wind, or how the body is formed in a mother's womb, so you cannot understand the work of God, the maker of all things. (Ecclesiastes 11:5)

> When nothing but a miracle will do, there's nothing that the hand of God cannot bring you through. I know He's more than able and he will deliver you-when nothing but a miracle with do.[2]

> Though he slay me, yet will I trust him. (Job 13:15)

> It's not my job to worry about tomorrow; it's not my job to say how it will be. I'm gonna lift my hands in praise for that's all He wants from me— not to figure out why the storm has come—that's God's job.[3]

---

[2] "When Nothing But a Miracle Will Do" written by C. Aaron Wilburn, as performed by the Arnolds.

[3] "That's God's Job" written by Rodney Griffen, as performed by Greater Vision, BMI.

Besides the scriptures and songs that meant so much to us, Kevin and I both received such an outpouring of concern from coworkers, friends, and certainly our families. We heard stories from folks that had gone through similar situations, and still others knew of someone that had a child that was diagnosed with a disease, and when they were born, the child was fine.

One day, somewhere in the middle of everything, I was sharing one of those stories with my boss, Judy Akins. After I finished, she told me about a conversation she had with God that morning as she was driving to work. She said she was praying to God to not let this happen to me and to let Karson be okay. His answer back to her was, "If I heal her, will you say that the doctors were wrong, or do I get the glory for healing her?" There is no doubt in my mind that it was God presenting her with the question. It wouldn't be the first or even the last time that he would speak to someone about us. My answer to that question was the doctors aren't wrong. I believed and had seen at least some evidence of that on the ultrasounds. I don't pretend to see half of what the doctors do on those things, but even I could see some of what they were telling me was wrong. I knew something wasn't right. So, yes, God would get all the credit if she turned out to be okay. But then I had to stop myself and say, "You know, even if he doesn't answer our prayers the way we want him to. He still deserves our praise simply because he is God." That is a hard truth to grasp at times, but nonetheless, it is the truth and maybe one of the greatest lessons I was to learn throughout this ordeal.

Years ago, I heard a preacher say two things that have stuck with me, especially in times of trouble. The first is this, "God will not parade his plans and purposes for our approval. We must never forget he is God. As such, he wants us to believe and trust him despite the things we don't understand." The second is, "Faith means believing in that which has no absolute proof. It is hanging tough when the evidence would have us bail out. It is determining to trust him when he has not answered all the questions or even assured us a pain-free passage." I certainly didn't understand his plan and there wasn't a day that was pain-free, but amazingly, there was some peace, and still is today.

Journal Entry from 4-19-03

You have really started moving a lot. In fact, I think you just learned how to do summersaults in my tummy. I love to think about you in there, full of joy and playing without a care in the world. At least one of us isn't worried about a thing. You keep me going when I think there is no way I can. I love you.

Maintaining the Persona of a Normal Pregnancy

On May 16, I had another ultrasound. We got the best picture of Karson's face. We could see everything—her eyes, nose, fat little cheeks, mouth, and chin. It was awesome. It made it all the more unbelievable that anything was wrong with her. I asked Dr. Stanley what he saw because to me, it didn't look like she was deformed at all. He said he really didn't see anything either. He thought there could possibly be a cleft palate and that her eyes might be a little far back in her head, but he didn't think she had any terribly noticeable defects. This only confirmed for me that God was doing a miracle with Karson. All the other pictures I had seen of babies with trisomy 13 or 18 had very obvious defects.

Journal Entry from 6-2-03

We went to see Dr. Stanley again this week. He said you were doing well. You weigh almost three pounds, and although your growth is a little behind, he was happy with your progress. We decided your birthday would be August 12, if everything continues to go the way it should. We also talked about goals for your delivery. I told him that if it turned out to be worst-case scenario, my goal was to hold you while you were alive. He agreed, so that means if you get into any kind of distress during labor, he will take you by C-section. He said a lot of doctors would think he was crazy to do a C-section on a baby that was terminal, but if my ultimate goal was to hold you while you are alive, he would do everything he could to make that happen.

Journal Entry from 7-2-03

We went to see Dr. Stanley yesterday. You weigh 4 lbs. 10 oz. Wow! You're catching up. You measured 32 weeks and 2 days. That is just a few days behind. The only change he found was that your kidneys looked a little large, but that's okay, it's just one more thing that God can take care of.

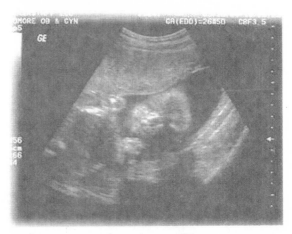

Journal Entry from 7-10-03

I don't know what it is, but today I feel an overwhelming love for you. Nothing has really changed, but suddenly, I am overcome with a sense of nurturing and the thought that you are my daughter, a part of me from head to toe is so strong. There is nothing I wouldn't do to protect you and show you how much I love you!

On July 26, Trish and my other wonderful friends that I work with threw a shower for Karson and I. Attendees were people from work and nearly all the women in my family. At first I had mixed feelings about letting them give us a shower. I didn't know if it would be something I could handle or not.

What finally made me decide it would be okay was the fact that if I believed in faith she was going to be healed, then she was certainly going to need some clothes and blankets and stuffed animals to play with. I found it to be a good decision for me. The one thing that I didn't do was decorate her nursery. Unfortunately, I guess my faith only went so far. We did have a crib, rocking chair, and tons of stuff for the nursery ready to go, but I just couldn't bring myself to put it all together. Instead, we just bought a bassinet and had it ready in case we got to bring her home. Since she would stay in it for a few months, at least it would give me time to fix the nursery then, if needed.

Journal Entry from 7-29-03

On July 29, I had my final appointment with Dr. Stanley before our scheduled induction on August 12. Dr. Stanley was leaving on vacation July 31 through August 7, so we wanted to be as sure as possible that I wasn't going to go into labor before he returned.

We went to see Dr. Stanley again. You weighed 5 lbs. 9 oz., and your heart rate was 146, and breathing motions were good. He said I wasn't dilated at all yet, but everything was looking good for the induction on the twelfth. We also had a great shower with all our friends in OKC today. Lots of wonderful gifts—you are set!

Our Miracle Takes Life

Journal Entry from 8-5-03

We went to see Dr. Becker today. Mommy has been having leakage and contractions today. Sure enough, he thinks my water will break soon; in fact, he was very surprised it hadn't ruptured already. You aren't too far from coming into this world to meet Mommy and Daddy face-to-face. (I'm excited about your coming early, in fact, I had a feeling you wouldn't wait another week. The only thing wrong with this is that Dr. Stanley is still on vacation. You were supposed to wait at least one more day—oh well.) Daddy was in Denver getting ready to leave on a trip, but he came home again. Grandma Koehn is also coming tonight just to be sure she doesn't miss your arrival. Grandpa is coming tomorrow. Everyone else is on alert.

When I called Kevin from Dr. Becker's office, he was about thirty minutes away from leaving on a flight. Instead, he just turned around and started home again. He had to fly into Dallas, so he wouldn't make it back to the house until 9:00 or 10:00 PM that night. My mom, who was also flying in, was getting into Oklahoma City about 10:00 PM. KaraLee and Chad Choate, Kevin's oldest daughter and son-in-law, volunteered to pick her up. I suggested to Kevin that we should just have them stay in Oklahoma City and we could meet them there, but he didn't seem very excited about that idea, so they all headed toward our house instead. At about 9:00 PM, Shelly Thompson and her husband Monty, friends that don't live too far from us, called to just check on me. When I told them that I thought I was in labor and that I was alone, they told me they would be right over. Ten minutes later, they were in our living room taking care of me. Shelly was great. She rubbed my back and helped me keep track of my contractions, which were kind of sporadic but getting closer as time went on. They thought we should go to Oklahoma City right away so that we were close to the hospital in case things started moving quickly, but I wanted to wait on Kevin. When he finally got there about 10:00 PM, I think he was a little surprised that I was actually feeling that bad. After watching me go through a couple of contractions, he agreed that it might be best to go to the city. Unfortunately, Kara and Chad were almost to our house by that time with my mom, so we just waited on them. They would have to turn around and go right back to where they came from.

Continued Journal Entry from 8-5-03

About 11 p.m. tonight, your dad, Kara, Chad, and Grandma Koehn and I headed to Oklahoma City to the hospital. When we got there, they put you on a monitor to make sure you were okay—you did great. My contractions were steady, but I hadn't dilated more than a one, and my water hadn't broken yet. So about 4:30 a.m., they released me. We all went to the hotel for a few hours of sleep.

I woke up with much stronger contractions the morning of August 6. We were supposed to go to the doctor later that morning, so I decided to get up and take a shower. I made it to the bathroom, and another contraction hit. Kevin found me bracing myself against the wall. He woke Mom up while I got into the shower. After I got out, I went and sat on the bed to get dressed when my water broke. I calmly told everyone we needed to finish getting ready and go to the hospital. I really didn't feel anxious or in too big of a hurry. I felt ready. Finally, the day had arrived when so many of the unknowns would be answered, and one way or the other, we were about to meet our daughter face-to-face.

I called Allison, by now a good friend, at the hospital and told her we were on our way. I also called Dr. Becker to let him know. He was in surgery, but they told me he would try to get there after that. What an amazing doctor he is. Since I was now technically under the care of Dr. Stanley, Dr. Becker had no obligation to be at Karson's birth, and yet he did everything he could to make sure he was there for me. When he arrived that day, he was a familiar face in a sea of mostly strangers, and just having him there gave me the assurance I needed to know we would get through this.

Kevin and my mom made the rest of the calls to the family to let them know. Kevin's nephew, Koll, was especially excited that it was time to go to the hospital. He kept telling everyone that they had to go because the baby had broken the water bottle. At the hospital, Allison met us and helped us get checked into the labor and delivery room suite. It was more like a hotel room than a delivery room. As we would soon find out, the room was just the beginning of one of the most incredible hospital experiences any of us had ever had. I am sure that some of the treatment my family and I received was because of my connection to the hospital and the fact that I am friends with some of the nurses, but certainly not all of it. I think, overall, the coworkers, nurses, doctors, and managers at Mercy Health Center just know how to treat people. They are in healthcare because it is what they love to do, and it shows. They literally became our angels of mercy for the next ten days.

If you have met the Bickerstaffs, you know that on the outside, they are pretty tough. In some books we might even be considered rednecks. I wouldn't go quite that far, but we probably are walking a thin line. Even that didn't seem to detour our caregivers. Allison made that clear from the very beginning. Anything we could dish out she could give it right back. For the situation we were facing, that was exactly what we needed. And it's as if they all knew it. Allison was just the first in a long line of unbelievable nurses. The next was Tena Ferenczhalmy, my labor-and-delivery nurse. When she walked into the room, with her smile that didn't quit, we knew we had someone special on our side. Again I'm sure I was not more important than any of her other patients, but boy did she make me feel like it. She made friends with each and every one of the family, and she anticipated our needs before we even knew what they were. She opened up and shared her own personal tragedies with us; when I got scared, she sat and cried with me, and when I needed to just be quiet, she would sit and hold my hand.

Before I went into labor, I thought I wanted to experience birth without any drugs to help me through it. After only a few hours of serious contractions, I was ready to give in. At first they gave me Stadol to take the edge off the contractions. When we hit the five-hour mark and I was only dilated to a three, an epidural started to sound really good. My rationalization to those who had been around me when I said I wanted to try it without one was that it was one thing if you only had to endure that kind of pain for a few hours, but it's a totally different story when you are potentially looking at twelve-plus hours. I applaud the women that do it. I guess I just thought I had a high tolerance for pain. Needless to say, I had the epidural.

Unfortunately, as the drug started to take effect so did some of the side effects. With the combination of my nerves, pure exhaustion, and the medicine hitting my body all at the same time, I began to get the shakes. At first if I put my mind to it, I could make it stop. But as soon as Tena would do another check to see how far along I was, it would start all over again. Every time I heard her say that we were getting closer to delivery, my fear escalated, and I couldn't control what my body was doing. After a couple of hours, I couldn't handle it anymore, and I asked Kevin to see if everyone would come in and sing praise songs with me. I needed the peace of God to come over me, and the music helped me focus on the good things instead of all the unknowns ahead. No surprise to me, it worked. It calmed my fears, and the shaking stopped, giving me a couple hours of relief.

At some time during the day, Dr. Reddy came in to talk to Kevin and me. He wanted to know what measures we wanted them to take to resuscitate Karson if she wasn't breathing when she was born. We decided we didn't want them to take excessive measures—no Code Blue, no respirators, etc. Nothing like putting a damper on what otherwise seemed to be a normal labor.

Thankfully we were not left to dwell on it for long. We had many visitors throughout the day and friends calling to check on our progress. Nearly everyone from Corporate Communications, the department I am a part of at Mercy, came by to see me and to see if they could do anything for my family. Everyone was so good to us. I know there will never truly be a way to repay all their kindness.

Interestingly, Kevin also spent some time at the mall that day. He had wanted to do something special for the family that was there with us to commemorate Karson's birthday. So he went shopping. He found the most perfect silver bell and had ten of them engraved to say, "Our little angel, Karson Grace Bickerstaff." For me, he picked out a beautiful silver plaque with a cross and a little girl on it praying. He had "We love you, Karson Grace Bickerstaff—Mom and Dad" engraved on it. He gave them to all of us that afternoon before Karson was born.

That evening, by the time I made it to a seven, the epidural had already started to wear off and the pain was becoming considerably worse. So the anesthesiologist gave me another small dose to get me through. Once again, the shakes seemed to take over my body. By the time I reached an eight, it was uncontrollable, and nothing I did made it stop. Then out of nowhere, I spiked a fever of 103 degrees. When that happened, things started to pick up pace around me. I don't remember much of what went on; I just remember hearing Tena talking to me every once in a while. When I came to the realization that I was no longer in control and I thought I was kind of losing it, I asked Tena to get Kevin for me.

Kevin had been in and out of the delivery room most of the day. He was still quite apprehensive about being there for the actual delivery. We had talked about this long before I ever went into labor, and we had come to an agreement. As much as I wanted him to be there, I told him I wouldn't pressure him. If he didn't think he could do it, that was okay. My mom and KaraLee were going to be there, so even though it wouldn't be the same, I would still have their support. On the other hand, he promised me that if it came down to it and I needed him, all I had to do was ask and he would be there. So when I asked, he came and never left my side again.

Kevin came in and literally lay down next to me in bed and held on to me, trying to get me to stop shaking so badly. I knew they had called the doctor and that he was on his way. I also knew that the baby's heart rate was escalating and that Tena was growing concerned. With all my might, I tried to stop the shaking. I kept telling myself to do it for Karson's sake, but nothing worked. Finally, at 11:00 PM, I was ready to push. Dr. Fred Coleman (Dr. Stanley's partner who was on call for him), Dr. Reddy, a team of NICU nurses, Dr. Becker, my mom, KaraLee, Tena, and Kevin were all there. This was it. The moment we had waited nine long months for.

Tena explained how to push through the contractions, breathing in three sets of ten each time. Kevin, Kara, and my mom all pushed and counted with us. Tena told me later that there were a couple of times she looked up and almost busted out laughing because all three of them were literally holding their breathes and pushing right along with me. They were nearly as exhausted as I was. We pushed and pushed. Then we pushed some more. It seemed to be endless. Kara must have thought it seemed endless as well. Every time she would count with me, she'd get a little faster. She was trying to get me through my sets of three as fast as possible so that I could rest for a minute before the next one started. It was, without a doubt, a group effort to get little Karson here. And I wouldn't have wanted it any other way.

I remember looking at the clock at 11:30 PM and them telling me we were getting close. Their *close* and my *close* were clearly two different things. I didn't know it, but I still had another good hour to go. At midnight, Tena let Dr. Coleman take over.

As we continued to push, there was a waiting room full of loved ones praying for us as they anxiously awaited word about Karson. It would be an injustice for me not to mention each of them by name because they too are part of our miracle: Kasi, Kevin's youngest daughter (at least for a few more minutes); Mandy McGuire, one of Kasi's friends; Jeanine and Bick, Kevin's mom and dad; Kevin's two brothers and most of their families—Kelly, Kathy, Koll, Kelsea, Kraig, Nita and Kasey; Bill Koehn, my dad; our good friends, Larry and Leann Spangler, Harvey and Tammy Wilson; and Chad.

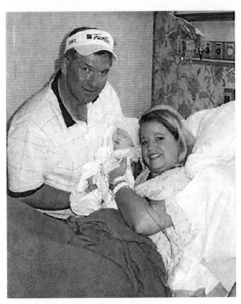

At 12:31 AM on Thursday, August 7, 2003, Karson Grace Bickerstaff entered this world.

When the doctor held her up for me to see her, all I could ask was, "Why isn't she crying?" My husband leaned over and told me she wasn't breathing and that she wasn't going to make it. The team of doctors and nurses performed normal measures (i.e., suction) with hopes that she might start to breathe, but after a few minutes and no sign of improvement, they wrapped her up in a blanket and handed her to me. So many things were going through my mind at that moment. I mostly remember thinking how beautiful she was. After all the speculation about what deformities she might have, she was perfect. There was nothing visibly wrong with her. She had her dad's nose, my lips and chin, two eyes and ears, a dusting of red hair, and ten tiny toes and fingers. She made a couple of gasps for air while we were holding her, but her doctor assured us that it was just a normal reaction to her body shutting down.

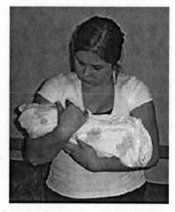

After a couple of minutes, Kevin said he would go tell everyone what was going on and bring them in to see Karson. As he left the room, I remember screaming in my head at God. I couldn't believe after everything we had gone through, he couldn't even answer my one request to let me hold her while she was alive. Was it too much for him to give me just an hour of her life before he took her away from me forever?

Kevin brought Kasi in first to see her little sister. I think that was when I really cried for the first time. She was so heartbroken. Silently, the rest of the group made their way into the room. I held Karson up for everyone to see and introduced her to the family she would never get to know. We wanted to give everyone a chance to hold her and to get a picture with her, so we passed her around from person to person. As we passed her, there wasn't much being said, a whisper here and there, lots of hugs, and a sea of tears. Every once in a while, Karson would gasp, but Kevin and I just explained to everyone else what the doctor had told us—it was a normal function of her body shutting down.

As Kasi stood holding her baby sister, about twenty minutes after she was born, she began to cry over and over again. We were all a little shocked. This didn't sound like a baby that was taking her last breaths of life. After a couple of minutes, the doctor finally came over to take a look for himself. He took her back over to the table and, after a few moments, exclaimed that she was indeed breathing on her own and had a strong heartbeat. This time, when they handed her to me, she cried, and I was sure I never heard a more beautiful sound in my life.

As my friend Allison would put it sometime later, just when you think God has let you down, the darned ole guy turns around and gives you exactly what you asked for. To this day, I don't know what to call what happened in that room other than a miracle. How else would you explain a baby not breathing for twenty minutes, and

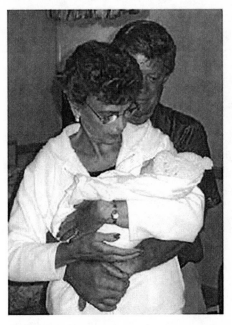 then suddenly, with no help from the medical world, she comes to life? I know, and I am sure the doctors would all agree with me, that this was not a normal occurrence. They were rendered speechless themselves. They could give us no explanation, and they had no idea how long she would go on without medical assistance. This was not something they could measure against history because in their books, it hadn't happened before. Who knew what this little girl might accomplish next. It was obvious God had something planned for her. We just didn't know what it was yet.

My dad sings in a group, and one of my favorite songs that they sing is called "We Have This Moment."

> We have this moment to hold in our hands, and to touch
> As it slips through our fingers like sand
> Yesterday's gone and tomorrow may never come
> But we have this moment today.[4]

---

[4]   "We Have This Moment Today" written by William J Gaither, 1975.

That song took on a whole new meaning for me that night. One of my other favorite parts of this story is about the people that we called right after Karson was born. I've never really asked them, but I love to imagine how they felt when they got the first phone call saying that Karson wasn't going to make it and then, a half an hour later, getting another phone call to say that she was alive. I picture it like it must have been in the Bible times when Jesus raised people from the dead—Jairus's daughter, the widow's son, and Lazarus. It says in Mark 5:42 that the people were astonished at what Jesus had done at the raising of the little girl. I imagine there must have been some serious celebrating taking place back then.

And surely, there was someone who jumped up and down praising God when he did the same for Karson. I know I was in my heart. This was our modern-day miracle, and Jesus may not have been there in the flesh, but he performed a miracle nonetheless.

Life After Birth

Now you'd think that after not getting more than four hours of sleep the night before, being in labor for fifteen hours, giving birth and being taken on the emotional ride of a life-time, my next thought would be to get some sleep. Nope, not this mom. After the nurses took Karson and bathed, weighed, and measured her (5 lbs. 11 oz. and 18 inches), we dressed her 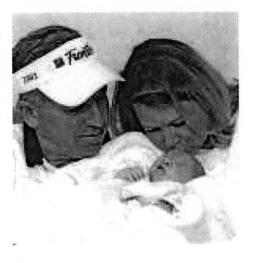 in a brand-new white dress and prepared for her first photo session. I don't just mean mother-in-law or sister snapping a few pictures with the family—I mean an honest-to-goodness professional photo shoot at two thirty in the morning.

Being the picture-taker that I am, I had made a verbal agree-ment with a professional photographer that we use at work, David McNeese. I had long since explained to him the situation with Karson and told him how important it was to me to have some good-quality photos of her soon after she was born. I warned him that it might mean she would not be alive but that I still wanted pictures. He agreed, and we actually had him tentatively scheduled to come to the hospital on August 13. When I went into labor early, my friend Tyler Thomas from work called and put him on notice. He said to call him day or night and he would come. I don't know if he really meant "the middle of the night," but being the awesome guy that he is, he came to the hospital at 2:30 AM. And he didn't cut any corners. We got the works—umbrellas, cameras, and lights. Karson was such a trooper through all this. I imagine if she could've talked, she would've said something like, "Gee, Mom, I've just basically come back from the dead, and all you can think to do is dress me up in an outfit that's five times too big for me and has an itchy collar and flash a bright light in my face over and over again. What's up with that?" After about an hour, she did talk to us, and she let us have it good. With her hands clinched in fists so tight you couldn't pry them open and a cry so loud it could've shook the rafters, she brought the photo shoot to an end. That was the first evidence that she had inherited something other than her father's nose. She had that Bickerstaff temper too.

Finally, at 4:00 AM, the nurses took Karson to the NICU. There they hooked her up to an IV to get her some fluids and also a heart and apnea monitor. With a promise to come get us if her stats changed at all, the rest of us decided it was time to get a little sleep. Some of the family went to a hotel, some went to the waiting room couches and floor, and some slept on the pullout couch in my room.

Slowly I started to feel the exhaustion take over my body, and I allowed myself to go to sleep. At 5:30 AM, the nurses woke Kevin and me and told us that Karson had had an episode where she stopped breathing for a couple of minutes. Because they didn't have a Do Not Resuscitate (DNR) order on hand, they had to do what they could to bring her back. They were successful, but now they wanted to know if we wanted to sign a DNR or if we wanted them to take excessive measures if it happened again. I was in no state of mind to make that decision, but somehow we both agreed to sign the DNR. They left us to go back to sleep, but after that, there was no chance either of us could sleep, so we got up and went back to the NICU to sit with and hold our baby girl.

At 7:00 AM, as I was holding Karson in my arms, the apnea monitor went off and her heart rate started to drop dramatically. With Kevin at my side, I told our baby that it was okay—if she needed to go, she could and that her mom and dad were there with her and that we loved her. I don't know how I did it, but a peace just came over me, and I knew I didn't want her to struggle. God had answered my prayer, and I knew that if I had to let her go, I would always have these memories. Thankfully, she recovered and continued to fight for her life. It happened again at ten that morning, but then things started to look up.

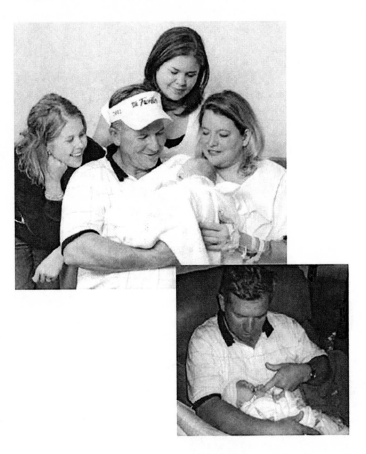

Appreciating Every Moment

After the three incidents that first day, we didn't have any more for a couple of days. Things were actually normal, as with any baby, except for all the monitors hooked up to her and the feeding tube in her mouth. For the first twelve hours or so, they kept her hydrated by feeding her sugar water. Finally, by the middle of the day on August 7, it was

clear that she needed more substance. They started feeding her 35 cc of formula every three hours. That made her happier, but it also gave her some serious gas. She seemed okay though. Once she would pass the gas, she would sleep calmly until the next feeding.

Between my husband and me and our family, Karson never spent a minute out of our arms except to change her diaper or for the nurses to check her vital signs. We would try to sleep when she slept, but for the most part, we stayed up with her day and night. Somewhere in there, we would sneak in some food and possibly a shower, but then we would be right back in the room with her. This was where the nurses broke the rules for us over and over again. Because of Karson's terminal diagnosis, they let us have someone in the room with her at all times. Normally, during shift change, there are no visitors allowed, but they made certain exceptions for us since we had no idea how long she would be with us. Which was a good thing because Kevin and I would've fought anyone who tried to get us to leave her alone, even for just a few minutes.

We had decided after her episodes that one of us would be with her at all times. If anything should happen, if not both of us, at least one of us would be there when she took her last breath.

On August 8, Dr. Reddy did his rounds and talked to Kevin about some of the tests they had run on Karson. They wouldn't have the results from the trisomy 13 test for about a week, but they had done some scans, and he explained what

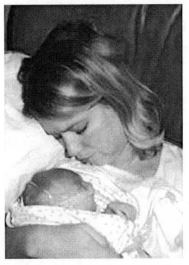

he thought some of the results were. Karson's kidneys were polycystic (a condition where the kidneys have become too big and may have many lumps), but he wasn't too concerned about them because she was having good urine and bowel movements. She still had the two holes in her heart and a valve that wasn't working, but for the moment, her heart was pumping strong. The most disturbing news was about her brain. Normally, the brain is divided into two distinct left and right brains. Her brain looked like it was all one unit. Even that didn't alarm us too much though because she was functioning so well. If you'll remember, Karson didn't breathe for a good twenty minutes when she was born. The fact that she was responding to anything was amazing in itself. She should have been brain dead, but she clearly wasn't. She could hear us, she sucked her thumb, she cried when we changed her diaper and when she was hungry—all things that do not happen if you are brain dead. Still, it was hard not to be disappointed with his report. But on the other hand, how could we be disappointed when God was doing so many incredible things with her?

That evening, Mike Packnett, the CEO of the hospital, came by to see Karson. He is such a genuinely caring man. He didn't stay long, but he took the time to pray with us. I was very impressed that he would even come by, and it meant a lot to me. My brothers both flew in the first couple of days as well. It felt so good to have so many of our family members close by with us. My sister-in-law Sophia and their kids, Kaliandra and Jakob, also tried to get to Oklahoma 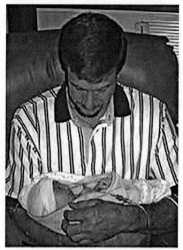 City to see us. Unfortunately, after sitting in the airport all day and not getting on any of the flights, they had to go home.

Karson seemed to have her days and nights mixed up. She slept most of the day and was more alert at night. But who could blame her? They chose 2:00 AM for her bath time and to do all her vital checks. Poor little dear.

On August 9, Karson developed jaundice, so we had to put her under the ultraviolet lights. That was hard for me. We had held her straight since she was born, and now we couldn't hold her at all. After some deliberation, however, they did agree to let us take her out and hold her for one half hour every three hours. I lived for this time. It was hard for me to share it with anyone else. I wanted to be selfish but tried to share her time as much as possible. So many people were there for us, and their love for Karson was so unbelievable. It only seemed fair they should get to hold her too.

Even though she was under the lights, we still didn't leave her alone. I stayed and held her hand, rubbed her forehead (something 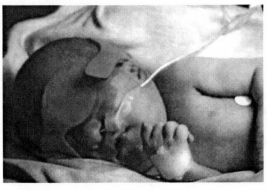 Kevin had discovered would calm her down when she was upset), sang, and talked to her. She had kind of a hard time at first because she was so used to being held. Her two grandmas had the idea to buy a CD player and some lullaby CDs so we could listen to music and maybe help her relax a bit. She had to wear these cute little blinders, which looked like purple sunglasses, to protect her eyes and nothing but her diaper. If you can imagine, she looked like she was in a tanning bed. It was actually pretty cute, as heartbreaking as it was. The next day, she was actually worse rather than better, so they gave her a belly light as well so she would have light from both sides.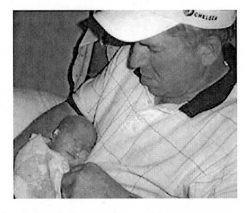

Dr. Reddy came by again and told Kevin that he and the radiologist had read the scans together, and they now believed that one of the holes in her heart had closed up and that the brain was indeed divided in two, just like it was supposed to be. Again, this was kind of unheard of for a trisomy 13 baby. At this point, all of us started to believe that God had healed her of this terrible disease, but we wouldn't know for sure until the tests came back.

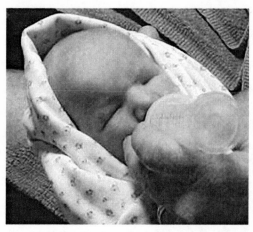

When Dr. Reddy told us this new information, Kevin and I discussed it and had them tear up the DNR. I actually was quite panicked that her heart would give out before the tests came back and she would die. Then we would get the results saying she didn't have trisomy 13, and all we would've had to do to save her was heart surgery. I couldn't bear the thought of it. We also decided to let them hook her up to oxygen. That in itself would not save her had she stopped breathing on her own, but it did make her more comfortable, and we were all about doing what was best for her.

August 10 was another day of firsts. Karson drank her first whole bottle, down to the last drop, all on her own. She also smiled for the first time. Right there, sitting with her dad eating, she smiled at him. We were so proud of her. Whatever the reason for the smile, it was just good to know she was happy and content, at least for a little while. She was also gaining weight. That night, when they weighed her, she was just a little over six pounds.

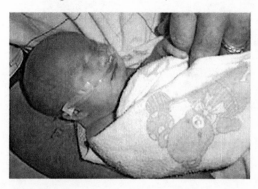

That evening, some friends of ours, Matt, Mickella, and Presley Smith from Ada, came to visit Karson. They told us the entire church service that day had been devoted to Karson.

Our pastor, Earl Hood, and his wife, Christy, had been up the night before, and we had given them a picture of Karson. They had the picture up on the big screen, and he told everyone Karson's story, and the entire church prayed for her.

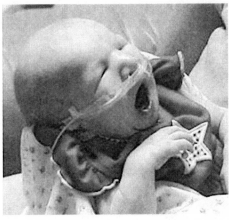

Kevin decided he needed to go home to Sulphur on August 11, to get more clothes, check on the house, and get the mail. While he was gone, I stayed with Karson the whole time and kept the phone close to me so that I could call Kevin if anything happened. Something did happen, but I didn't call him. The doctor that was on call that day, Dr. Sylvia Lopez, came in and abruptly announced to me that Karson's tests had come back earlier than they thought, and she tested positive for trisomy 13. There were no ifs, ands, or buts about it. She gave me the news and then left me alone to cry.

Kevin came in the room to see his little girl as soon as he got back. I kept trying to get everyone to leave so I could tell him about the test results. It was torture for me, but it took about thirty minutes before everyone finally cleared out. I just looked at him and told him the tests had come back. He knew right away what the results were. I didn't even have to say the words. Once again, we would sit in dis-

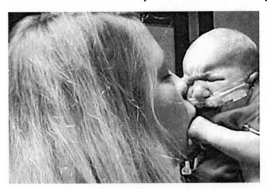

belief together and cry for our baby girl. I think we both believed with all our hearts that God had done a miracle and healed her. We were just waiting for the tests to confirm what we already knew. The news devastated us yet again, and if the truth be told, we were probably a little disappointed in God. Karson's jaundice was down quite a bit, but they wanted to keep her under the lights for another night. However, after we got 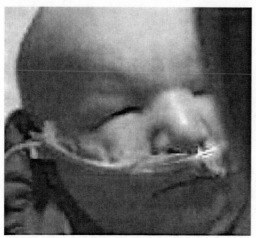 the news that day, they decided to let us take her out from under the lights and hold her. Her levels were back to a normal range, so they agreed that it was more important for us, and for her, to be able to hold her every second that we could from here on out. As this point, we couldn't have convinced a doctor to do heart surgery on her. We knew that would probably be what would end her life sooner rather than later. They told us there might be one or two doctors in the United States that would do heart surgery to repair the hole in her heart and the valve, but with a terminal diagnosis, no one in Oklahoma would do it. In a way I understood, but if it had given us even one more day with her, it would have been worth it to me at the time. Unfortunately, unless we wanted to try and find someone out of state that we could convince to do it, heart surgery was not an option. They knew her heart would probably be the first organ to go, but they assured us that if it wasn't the heart, it would soon be one of her other major organs. We had to believe them, and when it came down to it, we made the choice to just be with our daughter and spend every waking moment with her that we could.

One thing Karson hadn't done up to this point was open her eyes. No one really seemed too concerned about it. I thought at one point she might not have eyeballs, but Dr. Reddy said he had checked and she did have them; she just hadn't opened them yet. On Tuesday, August 12, while I was holding her, she opened her right eye, and we could see her pretty blue eye looking right at us. Kevin would talk to her, and her eye would move right to him. It was just one more thing that she had overcome, and we were so proud of her. She never really opened the other eye. She would get close sometimes but never quite got there, and she didn't open the right one very much, but as the days went on, she would do it more frequently.

On August 14, they took out Karson's IV and feeding tube, and we fed her strictly by the bottle. Dr. Ajay Verma (another one of her doctors) wanted us to try and get her used to the bottle feedings so that we could take her home by the end of the week. Saturday was our goal. Karson had to eat 40 to 45 cc of milk at each feeding. If she did that for twenty-four hours, then we could room in one night (spend the night in a regular room, not the NICU) and take her home the next day. Strictly bottle feeding her was a bit of a chore.

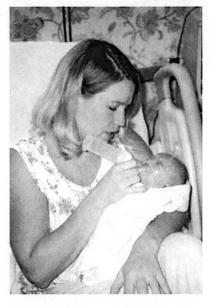

With everything unhooked, we couldn't simply finish what she wouldn't take by bottle with the feeding tube as we had been doing up until then. She had to drink it all by herself. She had a tendency to fall asleep after just a couple of sucks, so it was a process of waking her up over and over again to try and get her to eat. It got to the point that I would change her diaper right before we were ready to feed her because it would make her mad, and she would be awake for at least a little while. She hated to have her diaper changed.

I got another surprise on Thursday. My best friend from high school, Janice French, who now lives in Missouri, drove down to see us. I didn't know she was coming. In fact, I was quite sure she wasn't going to after talking with her on the phone. I had called her the day that Karson was born and had to leave a message because she wasn't home. When I finally did talk to her, I asked her how she was and she said she was very frustrated. As it turned out, she had planned to come to the hospital that next week when we were going to induce labor. When I called her, they had been at a youth function. Come to find out, they had stayed in Oklahoma City about five miles from the hospital the day after Karson was born. They just didn't know we were there until they got home and got my message. So, anyhow, she came to surprise us. It was so wonderful. It was one of the best days for me. It was really special to me to have her there and have her meet Karson.

Friday, August 15, brought us one step closer to going home. We were told we could move her to my room with us at 5:00 PM that evening. During the day, a representative from Mediserve brought the portable oxygen and monitor that we would take home with Karson. Kevin and I also decided we were going to take a quick refresher course in infant CPR. One of the nurses, Patty, took us in a room to go over the steps with us, and we started talking about why we were doing it. By the time we were done talking, we decided we didn't need to take the time away from our daughter to brush up on our CPR when we didn't plan to use it on her if she stopped breathing. Neither of us wanted to prolong her life when it came time for her to go. Our only prayer was that she would go peacefully and be in one of our arms. We didn't want her to suffer; she had already been through so much in her short life. It wasn't fair for us to be selfish with her; it needed to be about her needs, not ours. Doing CPR and bringing her back would only serve to better our lives, not hers.

That evening, we packed up all our belongings and moved baby Karson into room 630 with the rest of us. It was exciting but a little overwhelming at the same time. I was so scared I wouldn't remember all the things I had to know about the oxygen and the monitor and taking care of her. It's stressful enough just being a new mom, but the added stress of illness was something I wasn't sure I could handle at home on my own. There is something comforting about being in the NICU where the nurses can be there within seconds if needed. This was a test for us, but even in the room, we had a nurse that checked on us every couple of hours. The next day when we would take her home would be the true test.

Home Is Where the Heart Is

We brought our baby girl home on Saturday, August 16. It was a very hot, sultry day, but the weather didn't matter to us in the least. We thought we would be ready to leave the hospital as soon as Karson got released, but we quickly realized there was a lot more preparation that had to go into getting all of us home than just jumping into a car and going. Besides all of the accumulated clothes and stuff from ten

days of being away from home, we had a car full of gifts, plants, and flowers. In addition, we had three vehicles, six adults, and one baby with an oxygen and heart monitor to get loaded. My dad was also flying in about the same time we planned to leave the hospital, so someone had to get him as well. Emotions were a little high as we tried our best to get everything situated and figure out who was going where and who was driving what. To make matters worse, the hospital wouldn't let us leave without Karson in a car seat. We had a car seat, but it had been taken apart long before we ever went to the hospital and never put back together again, so when the time came to get Karson settled, we needed to get everything back in working order, and I couldn't remember what pieces went where. I knew that I was frustrating Kevin. He had been so adamant about leaving the minute the doctor released us, and it had already been three hours and we still weren't ready. Kevin happened to snap at me, at least in my mind he was snapping, about the car seat and how he couldn't believe I didn't remember how to put it together, and I had a little break down. While I was crying in the bathroom, they called the nurse to see if she knew how to put it together, and Kevin came to talk to me. I told him I was so sorry, and of course, he said it was no big deal. I was just so scared, and I was feeling pretty overwhelmed with everything we had to remember about the oxygen tanks and the heart monitor, the medicine and feeding Karson. There had been someone there with us twenty-four hours a day, and now we were going to be on our own

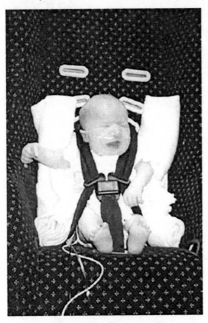

and expected to take care of a very sick little girl. I think I was most afraid of doing something to her without knowing it that would hurt her. I wanted to take her home, but I felt a lot of responsibility being put on my shoulders, and I was scared. We finally got the car seat put together and everything else loaded up on a cart, and we headed out to the cars. Kevin hooked Karson in the car seat as quickly as he could, all the while she was screaming at the top of her lungs. He herded the rest of us in so we could get on the road and away from the hospital. At this point, he wasn't really in that big of a hurry to get home; he just wanted us away from the hospital so I could take Karson out of the car seat and hold her. We no more pulled away from the curb and I had her out and back in my arms. I am a pretty big advocate for car seats, but not that day. She was so miserable in there. There is no way I would have ever made her stay in there all the way back to Sulphur. As Kevin drove us home, Karson and I fell sound asleep in the backseat and slept all the way to the house.

It was a good ninety-five degrees that day, so the trip from the car to the house was a quick one. We got situated in the recliner while

Kevin and the rest of the gang hauled all our things into the house. Our neighbor, Betty Andrews, came over shortly after we got home. She brought over presents, balloons, and food, and she showed us how to use the large oxygen tank that had been delivered for Karson the day before.

Karson adapted quickly to her new surroundings. We got her dressed in her little white tank overalls, and she was a happy baby just hanging out with everyone at the house. That afternoon the men took the kids out on the boat to go tubing for a while. I tried my darnedest to find the energy to get up and put things away, but I just couldn't do it, so, Karson and I spent most of the afternoon napping. We had planned to take Karson to the lake, but after realizing how hot it really was outside, we decided against it. It is one of my regrets now. The lake was such a special part of our lives that summer, and I wish we had shared it with her. Even though she might not have even known what was going on, I think she would've liked to ride on the boat and feel the warm air blowing on her. Had she lived, I think she would've been a real outdoors child. I can hear her now screaming at her dad, "Go faster, go faster!" What fun that would've been.

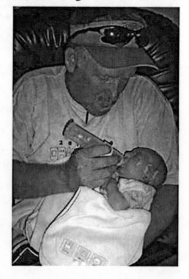

That night, we had quite a house full—my mom and dad, Kraigs, Kara, and Chad, Karson, Kevin, and I. During the day, they had put together Karson's bassinet for her to sleep in. We moved it into our room for the night, but when the time came to go to sleep, I couldn't

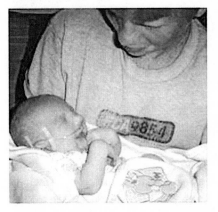

bear to put her down, so I just put a bunch of pillows around us, and she went to sleep in my arms, cuddled between her dad and me. It was just like we had talked and dreamed about for months. It was perfect.

The next day was Sunday. If all had been normal, we probably would've gotten Karson all dressed up and taken her to church. Since going somewhere with her entailed that we take along the heart/apnea monitor and oxygen, we decided not to venture too far from the house in those first couple of days. We had a doctor's appointment scheduled in Ardmore on Wednesday and thought that might be our first test for getting around with all her stuff hooked up to her. On Sunday, we got up around 10:00 AM. People were scattered throughout the house,

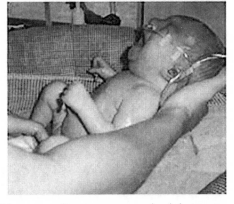

but generally in good moods. The guys all went out to the lake again for a while. While they were gone, we gave Karson a bath in her brand-new bathtub. She didn't like it any better than she did the sponge baths. As we were getting Karson undressed to take her bath, she peed all over herself and the monitor that was strapped to her (the monitor strap was absolutely not supposed to get wet). I am so thankful that my mom and Nita were there. They helped to calm me at times when I know that if it had just been me, I would have been hysterical with not knowing what to do. Our family continued to be a blessing day after day.

We had a number of visitors to the house on Sunday. Dr. Long and Trish came by after church and brought us strawberry cake. Rick and Rosie Hargis came so Rosie, who was with Mercy@Home, could check on Karson. Rosie checked her vitals and said she would be back in a day or so. Hospice was scheduled to come the next day, so we decided they would kind of trade off days for a while. Monty, Shelly, Jaylea, and Jaycea Thompson came to visit as well. The girls were so attentive to Karson and absolutely loved holding and doting on her.

By evening, everyone had finally gone home except for my mom, and we settled in to what we thought would be our routine for the next few days. We went to bed around 10:00 PM. I left Karson in her bassinet for a little while, but after about an hour or so, she ended up back in my arms for the rest of the night.

Monday dawned, and Kevin felt like he needed to get out of the house for a while, so he went to Ada to have breakfast with his buddies up there. Mom and I got up around 10:00 AM and took turns watching Karson while the other one showered and got ready. We didn't do much. It seems like we slept all the time, but I guess with all the emotions and waking up every three hours to feed her, it just got the best of us. That morning, Karson's apnea monitor went off twice, and the heart monitor went off once. It was evident to me that she wasn't having a very good day, and my heart was clutched with fear that we were losing her. Besides her labored breathing and heart problem, she wasn't eating more than a couple of cc at each feeding. I simply couldn't get her to eat no matter what I did. Finally, by the afternoon, I was so frustrated and at wit's end about how to get food into her that I started feeding milk to her with a syringe. My mom would fill it up, and I would squirt it into her mouth. It was a very slow process but the only thing that worked. At the point that we were doing this, my mom and I were so tired that we would fall asleep in between exchanges. Looking back, it is kind of comical, but I don't think either of us was laughing at the time.

Around three thirty that afternoon, I called Kevin and asked him to come home. I told him that she wasn't eating and that I didn't think she was doing well. While we were waiting on him to come home, the ladies from Cross Timbers Hospice stopped by to offer us their support. I remember we were all talking when Kevin got home, and he walked in, picked Karson up from my mom, held her up, and said, "Karson Grace, why aren't you eating? I'm going to have to whoop you if you don't start behaving better." Then he took her and hugged her close. As the ladies left, Kevin started feeding Karson her bottle, and do you know that she drank every last drop for him? And in record time no less. I couldn't believe it. If I had known all she needed was her dad, I would've called him a lot sooner and saved all of us some heartache.

The Moment of Truth

After Kevin had his dinner, he fed Karson another full bottle. I felt so much better about her, and I wasn't as afraid as I was earlier in the day. She seemed to be doing much better now that her dad was home and taking care of her. About eight thirty that evening, Karson and Kevin fell asleep in the recliner. Kevin was snoring so loud it rattled the windows, but it didn't bother Karson one bit. She just slept peacefully on his chest. I don't think I will ever forget the way they looked lying there together sleeping. It is one of my most prized memories.

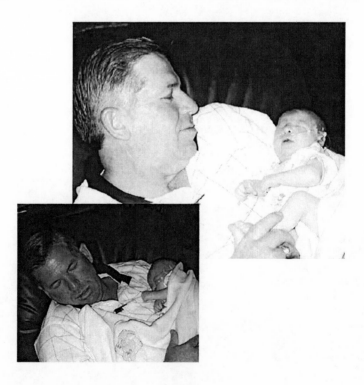

At about 10:00 PM, I woke Kevin up to go to bed. I didn't want to wake Karson, so I just left her in what she had been wearing that day—her cute little butterfly dress. Kevin asked me if I wanted him to bring the bassinet into the room for her to sleep in, and I told him I just wanted to hold her. I gave her a little bit of a bottle, and we all went back to sleep. At about 1:00 AM, I fed Karson again and changed her diaper. She seemed to be doing okay. We went back to sleep. About 3:00 AM, she woke up and was a little restless, so I thought I would try and feed her a little bit of her bottle. I changed her diaper first, and as Kevin got up to throw it in the trash, I started feeding her. Almost immediately after I gave her the bottle, the heart monitor went off. I tried to move Karson into a different position and get her to take a

breath. I told Kevin to try and reset the monitor, and I remember him saying it wouldn't matter if he reset it—if she wasn't breathing, then it would just keep going off, so the loud squeal continued as I tried to talk her into breathing for me.

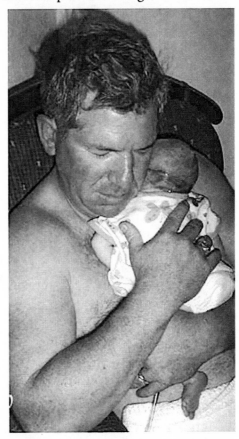

After about a minute, my mom came into the room. I handed Karson to Kevin and ran to get the suction tube. I thought maybe she was choking on the milk that I had started to give her, but that didn't make a difference either. Kevin was trying desperately to do something that would change whatever was going on in her body, but without any real hurried movements. It felt like we were moving in slow motion. He started to give her mouth to mouth, but just as soon as he started, he stopped. He put her over his shoulder and looked at my mom and me and said, "I think this is it, I think we're going to lose our little girl."

It was 3:10 AM on Tuesday, August 19. Amazingly, there were no frantic cries to do something; there was no running around trying to make the inevitable not happen. We just stood there watching as the angels came and took our little baby girl home with them. She didn't suffer, she didn't cry, she didn't even gasp for a last breath. She was just gone. Kevin sat down in the chair in our room and held Karson tight to him all the while the monitor was still ringing out loud.

After about five minutes or so, when we knew for certain that she was gone, I turned the monitor off and unhooked all the wires attached to her. Finally, she was free of all that had hindered her. At last we could hold her and know that she was perfectly well.

My Final Breath

I took my final breath
In my daddy's arms
I know he feels guilty
He couldn't keep me from death's harm

If I could I would tell him
It was meant to be this way
God called my name and sent the angels
On that very special day

My daddy wanted to save me
But there was nothing left to do
I went from his arms
To the one that created me and you

So don't worry, Daddy
Everything is okay
Take care of Mommy
And I'll meet you both in heaven one day

Going Through the Motions

Oddly enough, the next three hours or so, we took pictures of Karson, of each of us holding her and of all of us together as a family one last time. We even cemented her footprints. This was no easy task, and had it been under any other circumstance, it would've been quite funny. We first tried to do her hands, but they were in fists, and we couldn't get them to straighten out enough to imprint them.  Her feet were a little bit easier, but not much. We must have tried at least six different times before we felt like we had gotten an imprint that was good enough. By then, Kevin, Karson, and I had cement all over us. My mom and I gave her one last bath, and at 6:30 AM, I called hospice and asked them to send someone over that could pronounce Karson dead. Kevin called all of his family, and I called Trish and Judy. We dressed her in her little linen sailboat overalls and wrapped her in her blanket. Kevin called Criswell Funeral Home in Ada and told them that we would be bringing Karson. They offered to come and get her, but he was adamant about driving her to the funeral home himself.

Later on, we would find out that several different people had dreams or premonitions about Karson's death that night. My mom had prayed as she went to bed that God would heal her completely.

65

Her prayer was answered. Dr. Becker and his wife, Marty, were awakened at three fifteen that morning by the sound of a door shutting loudly as they slept. Dr. Becker got up to check it out and found nothing. As he walked back into the bedroom, Marty said to him, "That was baby Karson." My friend Janice had a dream that Karson had died, and she indeed had that very night. I don't know what to say about all these different occurrences other than they just affirm for me that it was her time to go. There was nothing we could've done to change the outcome. Kevin and I have both been racked with guilt since that night thinking that we should've been more aggressive in trying to save her. Why didn't we do CPR? We both knew how to do it, and Kevin even started to and then stopped. All I can say is that there was a peace about us, and it just didn't feel right to try and make her stay. As much as we wanted her to, it was time for her to be in the arms of God.

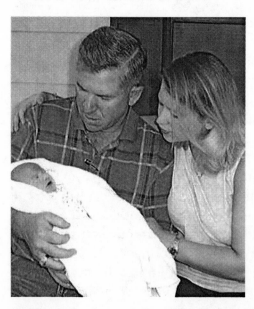

After we were both ready that morning, we picked out a dress to take to the funeral home, and we loaded up in Kevin's truck to start our last journey together. We called our pastor and asked him to meet us at the funeral home. My mom stayed at the house to get ready and do some cleaning since we knew we would have guests in and out over the next few days. The drive was probably the shortest drive we have ever made to Ada. I wanted Kevin to drive slower because I knew it was my last chance to hold her, and when we got to the funeral home, I was going to have to give her up physically for good. At the funeral home, Earl met us and took us in to meet with the funeral director. He talked to us about when and where we wanted to have the funeral and all the other details. We had decided early on that if and when Karson passed away, we wanted to have a funeral service with her there, but then we wanted to have her cremated so that we could always keep her with us wherever we went, so we also had to pick out an urn for her ashes while we were there that day. We picked out a bronze lamb. Looking back, I know without a doubt that, even then, in our deepest, darkest valley, God was with us. He was directing our decisions and giving us the strength to get through the day. There is no other answer. Without him, it would have been impossible. The next couple of days seem like a blur. I remember some of the things we did, but not everything. Some moments are etched in my mind forever—strange things like what I was wearing the day we took Karson to the funeral home—and yet I can't quite get the time frame all worked out in my head. Like for instance, after we left the funeral home that day and came home, I

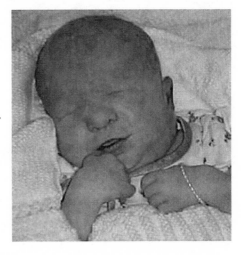

have no earthly idea what my husband did all day. I do know that Chad and KaraLee came over around noon, and my mom, Kara, and I went to Ardmore. We needed to print out some pictures of Karson for the service, and I wanted to get something to wear to the funeral. We must've been moving in slow motion though because at 8:00 PM, Kevin called me to ask when we were coming home.

I remember being emotionally and physically exhausted when we got back to the house, but I wouldn't let myself go to sleep. I needed to cut out the pictures, write the program for the service, and write what I was going to say on behalf of Kevin and myself at the funeral. I think I completed two out of the three before I just completely gave in to my body's exhaustion. The next morning, Kevin and I wanted to be at the funeral home as soon as they opened so we could be with Karson all day. I had missed her so much the day before. We had been with her constantly for twelve days, and then she was just gone. I couldn't wait to see her and touch her again. I

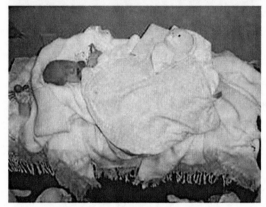

knew it was only her body and that it really shouldn't matter, but until you are faced with that situation, you have no idea how you are going to feel, much less behave toward your loved one. Kevin and I just wanted to be in her physical presence for another day. To sit and look at her with the hope that we never forget what she looked, sounded, and felt like.

Walking into the room at the funeral home for the first time was hard, but not as bad as I thought it would be. I wasn't sure how she would look or how we would treat her now that she was just the body of our little one. It was no different than had she been there for real. We gave her hugs and kisses, told her how much we loved her and how pretty she was. Other than being a little blue around her mouth, she looked the same, just like she was sleeping. I moved her hands up to her face so they would be positioned just as she had them every day of her life.

We had brought some stuffed animals, a rocking horse, her Bible, and her blanket to make her, and us, more comfortable. After we got it all arranged, we decided we needed some poster board to put all the pictures on, so we went to Staples to get some supplies. When we returned, Karson's grandmas were at the funeral home. We were also struck speechless by all the flowers that were arriving. Some of them from people we were barely familiar with. It proved to us again how easily Karson touched others and how her story traveled quickly to so many places and people. There were also names in the book at the funeral home that we didn't recognize. One name in particular was the lady where Kevin takes his dry-cleaning, Joyce Teal. She had come by when we were gone, and she just signed her name. We had no idea what her name was. We didn't figure it out until later that night. Kevin had dropped off some pants that morning to be starched, and he had told the lady about Karson. He was supposed to pick the pants up by 10:00 PM that night so he could have them for the funeral the next day. He forgot all about it until 10:15 PM when it all of a sudden hit him and he rushed down there hoping they might still be open. There sat Joyce waiting for him. She told him then that she had been to the funeral home earlier in the day, but there were other people there and she hadn't wanted to intrude. The nicest lady in the world, with a heart of gold, and we didn't even know her name.

We had lunch at a local hamburger joint, and then my dad and Glenn, Sophia, Kaliandra and Jakob arrived from Colorado. We all stayed at the funeral home for a while, and then Mom and I took them to Sulphur to check into their hotel, and I went to buy Kevin a shirt to wear to the funeral. That evening, the girls from work— Trish, Theresa, Janis, and Renee—brought a full course meal to the house for us. I stayed at the house until about seven thirty, and then I went back to the funeral home to say good night to Karson. I had a really hard time leaving her that night. I didn't want to leave her in a strange dark place all alone. I would've slept there, and seriously thought about it, if Kevin hadn't led me out by the arm. There were still quite a few people with us then, so we all went to JB and Edna Stalling's home from there. Edna had made BBQ for us, and we all sat around visiting for a couple of hours.

As we were getting ready to leave, my friend Janice Campbell, from Seattle, called and said she was just getting to her hotel. Kevin and I ran by there to see her before going home. What a sweet friend to travel all that way for us for one day and a very sad occasion. One of my regrets is that I didn't have her stay with us at the house. I just wasn't thinking when she had called to say she was coming in for the funeral.

When we got back to our house, Mike Neuharth, Kevin's friend from Minnesota, had also just gotten in, and KaraLee and Chad were there too. We stayed up and watched the video that KaraLee had gotten arranged for us, and she sang us the song she was going to try and sing at the funeral.  Believe me, there wasn't a dry eye in the room. Before I let myself go to bed that night, I finished writing what I was going to say at the funeral. Eventually, we all settled in for the night. I don't think anyone really slept well, but at least we got a few hours in before the next day arrived.

Letting Go — Karson's Memorial

August 21, 2003—the day we had to physically say good-bye and let go of our precious baby Karson. The day dawned hot and humid, just as expected. It was surreal getting ready that morning. I just kept thinking, "I'm getting ready for my daughter's funeral. How unbelievable is that?" It just didn't seem right, but as the minutes ticked by, we etched closer to saying good-bye forever.

I knew Karson was already gone, but to still be able to see and touch her was a great comfort. It made it all a little less real. But today was different. This was it. We would say good-bye and hand her over to the funeral home for them to take her away forever—at least forever as we know it on this earth.

Kevin, Mike, and I left before everyone else because we were going to the funeral home to see Karson that morning before going to the church. Kevin wanted to make sure they didn't cover her up at any time between there and the church. It's weird the things that become important to you in these times, but I think it is good to go with your feelings. There really is no wrong or right way in these situations. Others may not understand, but you have to remember, for people that have never lost a child, there is no possible way for them to comprehend what you are going through or, for that matter, predict how they would handle it should they be confronted with the same horror. They might even surprise themselves. At the funeral home, we went in and said good morning to Karson with hugs and kisses again. Janice met us there; and my brother, Donavon, and sister-in-law, Charlene, arrived while we were there waiting for them to pack everything up. Once they had all the flowers loaded up and ready to go, we let them take Karson, uncovered, to the church as we followed. We got to the church about fifteen minutes before the service was supposed to start, so the majority of people were already there. My wonderful friend Lisa Long and a bunch of other people were folding programs and handing them out. Amazingly, there really hadn't been any tears for me yet that morning. I think it was all too unbelievable and hadn't really set in that this was my daughter's funeral.

There were a lot of hugs and words of kindness, but I finally excused myself and went to the kitchen area to wait for the service to begin. I went to the bathroom and tried to fix my hair and makeup, but there was nothing I could do to make myself look okay. I remember wishing I had bought a different dress. I had decided on a tan-and-purple flowery sundress, and I looked more like I was going to a summer wedding than a funeral. I felt like the most inappropriate mourner. Nearly everyone else was in black. I don't know what I was thinking or what people were thinking about me. All I know is that it was an odd time to be worrying about it, but that was exactly what my mind focused on sitting back there by myself. Finally, Earl came and told me we were ready to begin. This was it. I knew Kevin was going to have a hard time from the very beginning because the song we had chosen to walk into was the lullaby version of "Swing Low," which he had sung to Karson over and over again in the hospital. We walked in arm in arm and sat down as the rest of the family filed in. I still didn't cry.

As far as funerals go, it was perfect. It was a beautiful tribute to our little girl. So much so that I really wish we would have videotaped it. I never in a million years would've thought I would want to watch it or relive that moment, but there was something so touching and even peaceful about it that I think I might have watched it again sometime.

Earl started out by saying a few words, and then they played the video with pictures of Karson from the past twelve days. I think I cried a little bit, but truthfully, I was too worried about Kevin and how he was holding up to think about what I was feeling. I didn't want to break down; I wanted to be the strong one. The song on the video, "I Believe" by Diamond Rio, was another song that had a lot of meaning wrapped up in it, especially for Kevin. After the video, it was Kasi's turn to speak. She read a couple of beautiful letters that she had written to Karson.

July 27, 2003

My baby Karson,

Though you aren't born yet, you and I have a connection. I cried the other day at the baby shower for you. I have yet to meet you, and I cannot wait until that day. You will be such a bundle of love. I'm so much older than you, so when it comes to you growing up, it will be more like I'm your aunt or something rather than your sister. At the shower, you received so many gifts that we aren't even sure you'll be able to use. The doctors have told your mom so many things that are negative, but she hangs in there with faith that could move mountains. My mom, on the other hand, pays no attention to what the doctors have to say and leaves you and all your fate in God's hands. As for Dad, I think he's scared; he's not a real big crier, but when it comes to you, me, and Kara, he's a completely different person. He's grown up a lot you know. I didn't know him real well when I was little, but you get the privilege of knowing him from day one. He'll be tough with you at times, but when you need someone to whine to, he'll be there too. You've got a wonderful mother. I've gotten the chance to get to know her as my stepmom, she treats me like I were her own. I can't wait until you meet her face-to-face. She'll be speechless. As for me, my little Karson, I love you more than anything. My name, Kasi Rae, means "little lamb." Not too long before you were born, you received a lamb that is so soft and plays music. Then you received a book that I opened up, and it read, "Lord, bless this lamb, this child." I cried because I want nothing more than for you to be okay and healthy. Dad says he had a dream the other night, and you were fine in it. God has mysterious ways of delivering messages to people. Honestly, there is no point in me even writing this; you won't be able to comprehend even the small words in this letter for at least another six to seven years, but it's okay. Don't worry about it. I just wanted to tell you some things, one of them being that I love you more than anything. Thank you for gracing us with your presence, baby Karson. I love you.

Kasi Rae
Your sister

They say miracles come when you least expect it. Karson was a miracle. She surprised every doctor, every nurse, and every negative thing that was said about her health. She was just a miracle. I think she knew she wasn't supposed to hold on that long, so she pulled that Bickerstaff blood through and fought to the very end. She was our angel. God did not put us here to be sick; he put us here to live long lives in his name. Sometimes though I think he wants to remind us of how easy he can talk to us. Karson, I think, was his angel he sent down to bless us. Within just twelve days, she touched so many lives. People who had never met us before were praying that God would provide a miracle. Although it may not always be what we want, God always has a plan. Karson was a miracle the moment she began to breathe. Every single breath she took just shows how much power he has. And as for the nurses and the staff working at the hospital, though they saw the true orneriness of the family, they were blessed too by our little Karson. She was our angel sent in disguise.

After Kasi was done reading her letters, at my request, she sang "Jesus Loves Me" a cappella. She just belted it out. It was amazing. It was my turn next. Maybe this was why I was holding back the tears. I didn't want to get up there and not be able to get through what I had to say.

> On behalf of Karson, Kevin, and I, I want to express our gratitude for the outpouring of love shown to us and our baby girl over the last two weeks. Each of you has touched our lives in different and special ways. From the food to the flowers to the visits, phone calls, and cards—your support has been nothing short of overwhelming. There are no words sufficient enough to thank you. Our only hope is that some day in some way, God will bless your lives as much as he has ours.

> We would like to extend special thanks to our family members who have stayed with us day and night since Karson was born. There wasn't a time that Karson was not being held, kissed, snuggled, and sang to. There is no doubt that she felt loved, and nothing was more important to her dad and me than for her to feel loved. You went above and beyond what would be expected of any family, and you have touched our souls to the core. You never gave up on Karson, and in turn, she gave us twelve of the best days of our lives. Everyone seems to have an opinion about who Karson resembled, well, she may look like Kevin and me on the outside, but there was a little bit of each of

you inside of her. She was a fighter and an angel all wrapped into one. We will never forget her, and we will never forget the part that each of you played in her life. Thank you.

Standing here today, it doesn't feel like God answered any of our prayers, but both of us know Karson received the ultimate healing Tuesday morning, and we praise God for the time we were able to have with her. She truly was our little miracle from start to finish.

There is so much more I wish I could've said that day. If I had thought I could make it through, I would've personalized it more, instead of encompassing everyone into one big thank-you. So many people brought so much to Karson's life, and they deserved to be acknowledged and thanked if that is even possible. I'd like to take the time to say now what I didn't get to say then.

Kasi—What a precious bond you had with Karson. I do believe we saw hints of you in her from the very beginning. She was so strong, but she also had a big heart. How appropriate that you should be the one holding her when she took her first real breathes of life. She gave you a gift that day, telling you how special you are and to never give up on life—it's worth fighting for. And when you don't feel like you can make it on your own, connect with those that love you. She's watching over you, Kasi, and she's just as proud to call you her big sister as I am to call you my daughter.

KaraLee—For such a petite little thing, you sure have a lot of strength. You never gave up on God, and I know you believed with all your heart that he would heal her. Even when she died, you didn't waiver in believing God was in control. Thank you for taking so many pictures of your sister—because of you, we have chronicled nearly every minute of her life, and we will treasure those captured moments forever. You were everything that a big sister should be and more.

Chad Lynn—Karson would've loved you, just as we all do. Thank you for being around so much, for the many airport runs, and especially for adding humor in the toughest of times. You provided us some serious stress relief just by being you.

My mom and dad—"Finally, brothers, whatever is true, whatever is noble, whatever is right, whatever is pure, whatever is lovely, whatever is admirable—if anything is excellent or praiseworthy—think about such things" (Philippians 4:8). I can't think of two people this verse describes better. You are such shining examples of mind over matter, and I like to think I learned at least a little bit of that from you. Thank you for being there for us and for Karson. You did exactly what grandparents are supposed to do—love and spoil your grandchild. Mom, your presence during Karson's birth, every day of her life, and at her death means more to me than I can ever say. You were constantly there to pick up the pieces and encourage me as a first-time mom. You took over the mundane jobs that had to be done and sacrificed so that I could spend every possible minute with my daughter. The time I was allowed with her was more because of you. Dad, thank you for teaching us how to handle death with grace and accept it as part of the journey. I don't know that Kevin and I will ever get to where you are, but you sure give us something to reach for.

Donavon and Glenn—I didn't expect you to come after Karson was born, but I wasn't surprised that you did. It meant the world to me that you would fly out to meet your niece. You touched a place in my heart that has been, and will always be, reserved for you, my brothers.

Sophia, Kaliandra, Jakob, Charlene, Skyler, and Dillon—With all my heart, I wish you could've gotten here when Karson was alive. I know it wasn't for lack of trying, and I know that your hearts were breaking not to be here. Praise the Lord we will get another chance someday—one where sickness and full airplanes will not even factor into the equation.

To the rest of the Bickerstaff clan—As you all know, I come from a very different background than you do. Before everything with Karson, I would've considered my family to be the calm, caring ones and you to be the fun and rough ones. But I see you in a whole new light now. When times got tough, you were the ones there day and night. You waited through fifteen hours of labor, and then you basically hung out in the hospital waiting room for the next ten days, and then you followed us home. Never in a million years would I have envisioned you there with us the entire time, but I wouldn't change it for anything.

Jeanine—Your willingness to do anything that was needed—from getting us food, buying me clothes, to watering the plants and flowers, to sitting with Karson while we showered and ate occasionally—you were there endlessly, and your sacrifices did not go unnoticed. If you hadn't been there when the not-so-nice doctor bluntly told me that Karson's tests had come back and she was not going to live, I think I would've died right there on the spot myself. You have a knack for being in the right place and the right time with the best of hearts.

Bick—You touched my heart deeply the day you hung Karson's ultrasound picture on the wall of your restaurant. Your ways of show-

ing love are sometimes a little more subtle than others, but no less powerful. Karson would've loved hanging out with her Papa Bick, and I just know she would've been your little sugar.

Kelly and Kraig—Believe it or not, it's your tenderness

that got me. It didn't surprise me that you were there for Kevin and me, offering your support in any way that you could, but seeing you hold and talk to Karson will be a memory engraved on my heart forever. I didn't know you had it in you, but believe me, I will never forget it or question it ever again.

Kathy and Nita—You are such special sister-in-laws and friends. You are very strong women, and Karson would've learned a lot from you, just as I have.

Kris, Andrea, Kasey, Kody, Koll, and Kelsea—I am so glad that Karson got to meet each of you, her cousins. She was one of you and always will be.

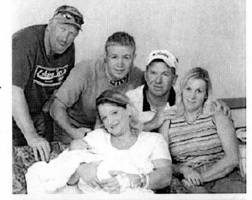

My best friends Janice F. and Janice C.—You two are the greatest. When one wasn't there, the other one was. You each have qualities as mothers I hope to one day possess, and as friends, I could search the world over and never find anyone better. Even through the distance, you managed to comfort and encourage me, and at just the right times, you showed up in

person. Thank you from the bottom of my heart.

Mike—I wasn't privy to all the phone conversations you had with Kevin over the last few months, but I do know you can encourage and lift his spirits like no one else can. There's never been any judgment, just friendship. Your being here is a highlight for Kevin, and if ever he needed one, now is the time. Thank you for being his brother and our friend.

JB and Edna Grace—One of my deepest regrets is that Karson didn't get to meet you. I hate it and would do it over again right this time if I could. But there are still many thank-yous to be said to the two of you. JB, do you know you are one of the only people that ever told me during my pregnancy that I looked pretty every time you saw me? That simple statement was so uplifting to me. Edna Grace, we chose you as Karson's namesake for so many reasons. Kevin and I count you as one of God's greatest blessings. You mean so much to us. Your strength, generosity, and sweet spirit are just a few of the characteristics that make you so special. We are so proud to have had a little girl that we could name after you. Although she is yet to meet you, we know that she is looking down on us and is honored to share her name with such an incredible lady. Thank you for simply being you. We love you both.

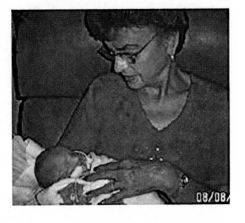

My friends and coworkers—You made our hospital experience one of ease and, surprisingly, one of joy. Because of your great spirits of mercy, you were able to meet all our needs in a very special way. I know I never would have been as relaxed or able to totally focus on my child without you. You shared your time, energy, and talents with us in very unique and special ways. Each of you holds a special place in our memories of Karson.

Lisa Long—Thank you for keeping me clothed. I would've been in the same clothes daily if it hadn't have been for you. Going through pregnancy at the same time as you and leaning on you for advice was something I really came to rely on. Your friendship means the world to me.

Tyler Thomas—Thanks for creating Karson's beautiful memorial handouts and for agreeing to do her announcements. You are so talented, and the fact that you would so graciously take it upon yourself to do those for us is beyond the call of duty—it was pure friendship.

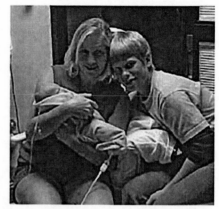

Nancy and Paris Woodard—Thanks for the wonderful fruit smoothies. I came to look forward to your visits each morning, and I needed them desperately. I also know that the two of you spent a lot of time talking to God on our behalf, and I know he heard each one of your prayers.

Sheri and Judy—Thanks for being such prayer warriors for us and for constantly providing our family with meals.

Mary Harris—Thanks for picking up where I left off at work. You have no idea what a relief that was to me not to have to worry about it. You are such a bright spot in my life.

Trish Long—Thanks for being the one with the shoulder for me to cry on. Your sympathetic ear was what I needed most at times. You will always be Karson's Mimi and one of my dearest friends.

Earl Hood—Thank you for being there with us at the end of our daughter's life and for making this day as easy as it could possibly be for us. You are much more than just a pastor to us.

To Kevin's Frontier family—I don't think anyone is here in person, but I know many of you are here in spirit. You have been a godsend to us. Thank you for opening your lives to Kevin and for sharing in his grief with him. Your support came in ways we never expected and never can repay.

There are so many more of you that deserve our gratitude. I wish I could do more than merely mention your names, but I hope you know in your hearts that you were as big a part of Karson's life as the rest of us: Betty Andrews; Dr. and Mrs. John Becker; Chris Fair; Rick and Rosie Hargis; Linda Herndon; Christy Hood; Dr. Larry Long; Teresa Matthews; Michele McEver; David McNeese; David and Ronda Meadows; Mike Packnett; Janis Preston; Renee Sandvick; Audrey Seiling; Larry and LeAnn Spangler; Matt, Mickella, and Presli Smith; Dr. John Stanley; Larry Stellman, Sr.; Carolyn Stoutz; Joyce Teal; Monte, Shelly, Jaylea, Jaycea Thompson and Harvey and Tammy Wilson; and the nurses at Mercy NICU. Every time we remember Karson, we will remember each of you.

Finally, to my husband—You are my rock. I know you don't feel like it, but there is no way I could even stand up here without your love and strength supporting me. We have both encountered something in our lives that we never expected to have to go through, and in truth, the awesomeness of it is bigger than both of us. It has enough potential to crumble and threaten our daily lives with fear  and anger, but together, we are making it. Somehow, we will get through this and go on, all the while knowing that we are better for the love and life of Karson than we ever would have been without it. Our little angel bonds us together in a way not very many people will ever experience. And there is a blessing in that. I know that even though Karson only had physical life for twelve days (and the nine months growing inside of me), she knew she was loved. She knew our voices, and she was comforted by them. And sure enough, she was Daddy's little girl. You could get her to do things for you that I couldn't, and I know she felt safe and protected cuddled up next to you. Even though doubt assails me at times, in my heart of hearts, I know as her parents we did everything conceivable there was to do for her. We fought for her life, and we didn't give up until God said it was time. There is no place she would have rather been than in your strong arms when she went to be with Jesus. She never had to be afraid because she went from her daddy's arms straight to that of her Heavenly Father. What more could we ask for?

That's what was really in my heart and what I would've said had I had the strength to get through it that day.

Next up on the funeral agenda was my dad. He wasn't originally going to speak, but before the service began, he asked if he could say a few words. I'm so glad he did because it was a true blessing.

> Karson amazing Grace. How sweet the sound. An angel came to us, and her name is Karson Grace. She chose the most worthy woman that could be found to bring her here, and the Father is so proud of her. Karson Grace told us from the beginning that she would be a very special angel and wouldn't stay but for a moment—just long enough to show each of us what pure unconditional love can do in this world.
>
> Family and friends held her close so as not to miss what she had to say. Karson Grace lived her purpose to the full and then went back home, leaving us with tears of which each drop is a precious memory. Let us live the love she so lovingly shared, and who knows, Karson might invite us to her home someday.

The final thing before Earl closed was KaraLee singing "The Masterpiece."* She wasn't sure she would be able to go through with it, and she had her mom standing by as backup just in case, but true to her form, she got up there and sang beautifully for her little sister. It was as if the song was written just for her.

> Before you had a name or opened your eyes or anyone could recognize your face you were being formed so delicate in size, secluded in God's safe and hidden place.
>
> With your little tiny hands and little tiny feet and little eyes that shimmered like a pearl, he breathed in you a song, and to make it all complete, he brought our masterpiece into this world. You were a masterpiece, a new creation he had formed, and you were soft and fresh, like a breezy summer morn. And I'm so glad that God decided to give you to me, my little lamb of God—you were a masterpiece.
>
> Surviving was not easy; your short life was a miracle. Every time I looked at you, I stood in awe because I saw in you a reflection of me. And you'll always be my little lamb of God.
>
> And as our lives go on each day, how I pray that you will know just how much your life has meant to us. It is so hard to let you go, what else is there to say, you were the masterpiece he created you to be.[5]

As everyone filed out and said their good-byes to Karson, I remember thinking this can't be over yet. I wasn't ready for it to be

---

[5] "Masterpiece" written by Gloria Gaither, Brent Alan Henderson, Craig Patty, and Michael Patty.

over because every step we took meant we were getting closer to the final good-bye for us.

Kevin and I were the last ones to leave the sanctuary, and as we walked through the doors at the back of the church in the foyer, I was overwhelmed with emotion. There stood all our friends and family in one big circle waiting for us. That kind of summed it all up for me. There they were, just as they had been for months now, waiting to see what they could do for us, how they could support us next.

Our Final Farewell

We invited everyone to stay and eat. The wonderful ladies at the church had prepared a veritable feast for us. Not many stayed, but it was a comfortable crowd. After about fifteen minutes, the funeral director came and told us they were ready to take Karson, so Kevin and I and a couple of others walked back into the sanctuary where she lay. My friend Janice held her for a little bit and then gave her to me. I think a few people stayed close by, but to me, everyone disappeared except for Kevin and the child in my arms.

Kevin kissed her and told her good-bye, and then I put Karson right up to my face again—nose to nose, just like when she was born—and basked in the miracle of her for just a few more minutes. Kevin finally had to urge me that it was time to let go, so I covered her with kisses and said good-bye. He took her from me and laid her back in her little casket. We started to walk out, and I looked back and saw her lying there all by herself, and I couldn't do it. I told Kevin I needed just a few more minutes with her, just one more kiss. So we went back. By this time, I was near hysterics, and I told him I couldn't do this. I couldn't leave her. He gently put his arm around me and led me out the door, not allowing me to look back a second time.

What a defining moment in my life. The ultimate test of letting go. I really can't imagine anything more difficult. I think having endured this pain, there is nothing I couldn't handle if presented with it. God took us to the brink, let us fall, but then as we would soon realize, he would pick us up again.

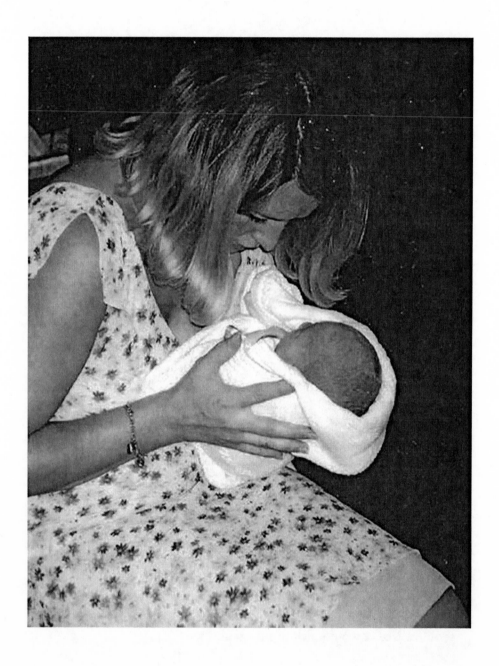

For the rest of the day, our families fellowshipped together. We stayed at the church for a couple more hours then went to our house. As it often is after funerals or tragic events, we hungered for laughter. We all sat around telling jokes, beating up on each other, and listening to the "Blue Collar Comedy" CD.

By about seven that evening, people were dwindling and I was so exhausted that I lay down in the bedroom. I woke up a couple of times to say good-bye, but then I slept through the night. That's another one of God's blessings. He got me through the nights. I know if I had woken up a lot, my mind would've started thinking about where she was, and it would've driven me crazy. Thankfully, I only had to deal with those thoughts during the day, but they seem easier to cope with in the light than in the dark of night.

Before my sister-in-law Kathy left that night, she said she had to tell me something that Kelsea had said to her at the church. While the adults were sitting around visiting after lunch, Koll, Kelsea, and their younger cousins were entertaining themselves by exploring all over the church. After a while, Kelsea came and got Kathy. She took her by the hand and asked her to walk back to the sanctuary with her. Outside the sanctuary, she asked Kathy if Karson had already gone to heaven. Kathy reminded her that they had talked about Karson going to heaven. Kelsea then said, "Yes Momma, she has gone up to heaven! I know because I went in there to check on her, and she's not there! She went on up to heaven while we were having lunch." Obviously, the funeral home had taken Karson's body with them from the sanctuary after the service, but as far as Kelsea was concerned, she was gone because she had to get on up to heaven. Oh, to be that innocent. Out of the mouths of babes come beautiful truth and understanding.

After the Storm

The next day, we planned to take my brother Glenn and his family to Turner Falls so the kids could swim and play in the waterfall. Before we left, I went to put some cat food out and found a possum in the garage. I went and told Kevin. I don't know if it was a good or bad thing, but it provided him with a mission. I can still see him running across our backyard, gun in hand. He shot at it and hit it, but didn't kill it. He finally caught up with it and proceeded to beat the life out of it with the end of the shotgun. I knew it wasn't the possum he was mad at; it just happened to be the poor victim in the wrong place at the wrong time.

The outing at the falls was a good outlet for me, but it was hard for me to watch the families with babies that were there. As hard as it was, though, I couldn't seem to tear my eyes away from them. It's still that way even today. I keep thinking that should be me with Karson or that should be Kevin with Karson. I wonder why we were the chosen ones to go through this rather than someone else. That evening, we drove to Marlow to watch a football scrimmage. I don't think any of us really wanted to go, but we had planned to take Karson there on her first big outing had she lived, so we decided to go anyway. It was especially good for Kevin. He likes to be around people, throw himself into something other than his grief. I'd rather wallow in mine for a while, but this was still about supporting one another, so off we went. I had one break down during the game, but all in all, I think I did pretty good. And that's how it was for a while—going through the motions one day at a time.

Our Little Lamb

On Saturday, two days after the funeral, we went to pick up Karson's ashes at the funeral home. I think we were both expecting something bigger than what they handed us. The little lamb urn was just her size. It hadn't occurred to me that it wouldn't be very big because she wasn't very big. We got the rest of her belongings and headed for home. At home, we took the ashes out of the urn and inspected them. I guess curiosity got the best of us.

That afternoon, Kevin went to Marlow to check on our newly acquired rock shop, and I stayed home to go through Karson's stuff and put it away in the cedar chest. As I went through her things, I, of course, shed a lot of tears, but I also talked to her and to God. And I know in those moments, she spoke to me too. I heard her tell me, "It's okay, Mommy, I'm okay." And I felt at peace.

On Sunday, we took Koll and Kelsea to meet their parents (they had stayed over with us since the funeral). We agreed to meet Kelly halfway. As we took off, we left Karson (the little lamb still lovingly referred to as Karson) sitting on her cedar chest surrounded by her things. That would be the last time we would do that. I felt like I had abandoned my child all over again. And when it got dark, it really troubled me, so we made a pact to take her with us everywhere we went from there on out. Eleven months later, we still take her everywhere we go. To us, the little lamb is all that we have left besides our memories, and it makes it easier to have something tangible to hold on to. I know Karson is not here. She in heaven, and this is merely the remains of her body and the shell that now houses what she once was; nevertheless, this way, she is still a part of our everyday lives. I expect that even though the pain will ease as time elapses, it won't ever completely go away. I don't know that I want it to. She is part of our family, and I don't want a day to ever go by that I don't think about her.

Reflections of My Soul

Karson was, like every child, a miracle from start to finish. Remarkably though, she was able to teach me more about God and my own strength and faith than anything else ever has up to this point in my life. She taught me that miracles come in many shapes and sizes. I also learned that God's miracles and our miracles may not always be the same thing, but it is worth every trial and tribulation to put your trust in him. He is the author of all life, and with his strength and guidance, I am empowered to make it through even the toughest times in life.

We recently celebrated what would have been Karson's first birthday and the anniversary of her death. It's hard to believe it's been a year. Some days it feels like it was just yesterday that we were holding her, and at other times, it feels like ten years has passed. One thing I have realized is that the blessings I have taken away from my experience and the lessons I learned don't end just because she is gone. I am still gathering life experience from something that happened over a year ago, and I suspect since it is embedded in my heart forever, I will continue to find new things to reflect upon and treasure as I mature and especially as I go on to have more children.

Grief Comes in Many Shapes and Sizes

There are several things that have really helped me deal with my grief and to move on with my life since Karson passed away. One of those things is to understand that no one grieves in the same way. In fact, Kevin and I grieve in totally different ways, and as time moves on, we realize more and more how blessed we are to have accepted that difference in each other. It has brought us closer rather than farther apart.

Not more than a week after Karson died, Kevin and his brother bought a decorative rock business in the town they grew up in. They had been talking about it a month or so before Karson was born but thankfully decided to hold off to see what transpired with Karson before jumping into a new business venture.

Admittedly, I was not thrilled with the idea either before or after Karson, but he bought it anyhow. He completely threw himself into making it a successful business. From morning to night, it consumed him. It was either that or be consumed by the aching in his heart. Fortunately, I think it turned out to be a good decision. Kevin works like a madman when he is at the shop, but he also has to spend a lot of time on the road since the business is located about eighty miles from where we live. The time spent on the road has been good for him. It allows him the quiet time he needs to wrestle with the feelings in his heart and time to talk to Karson one-on-one. Then he can go about his business and let go for a while.

I, on the other hand, spent a lot of time alone after Karson's death, not doing much of anything. Some days I would go with Kevin, but I really wasn't ready to face people. If I had done exactly as I had wanted to do after the funeral, I would have packed my bags and headed for the beach somewhere to write. But again, Kevin and I had to come to a compromise. He didn't want to come home at night and be alone, and he wanted us to at least be within driving distance of one another for a while. For him, there was great comfort in knowing we were there for each other. Don't get me wrong, he was a great comfort to me too, but there was so much raging in my heart that I needed to let out, and I wanted to escape to a place of inspiration and write about my feelings without interruption. The compromise was that I stayed home for the two weeks after Karson died, and then when Kevin went back to flying, I went on my getaway trip.

That's where I started this book. It began as an outlet for me to express my feelings, a way for me to remember every day of Karson's life and how it felt to go through it, but it turned into even more than that. I don't know who, if anyone outside of our family and friends, will ever read this, but if it can touch someone else's life and make a difference, then it means that Karson's legacy lives on.

Dr. Stanley mentioned to me a few months after Karson died that he would really like to have something he could give parents when confronted with situations similar to ours. Before they made a decision to end a pregnancy because of the possibility of a bad outcome, he wanted to be able to give them the perspective of someone who had been through it and had come out blessed on the other end because of the conscious decision to carry on. If that person is you, if you get nothing else out of this book, please know this: all the pain in the world was worth it the minute I held my daughter in my arms. Even if she had never taken her first breath, it would've been worth it, and I would do it all over again in a second.

God's Plan

I hope our story can help you, whether you are facing a troubled pregnancy; suffering from the loss of a loved one, young or old; or just questioning why God allows bad things to happen to good people. As much as I pray I never have to go through such pain again, I also wouldn't trade one moment of what we went through. The thought that I could've ended my pregnancy and missed out on the blessing of my child makes me sick at my stomach. What incredible things we would have missed out on. It might have been the easier choice, but no one ever said life was going to be easy.

In fact, if you believe in God, you know he promised exactly the opposite. We are guaranteed trials and tribulations in this life, but thankfully and mercifully, God has promised to be there with us through it all.

"And we know that in all things God works for the good of those who love Him and have been called according to His purpose" (Romans 8:28). I will not pretend to know why God allowed us to lose Karson or to ever go through that kind of pain, but I am certain he was in every decision, every doctor's appointment, every moment of fear; and he is the only reason I can sit here today and write about the blessings that came from the life and death of our daughter. It's easy to understand the blessings her life brought about. It is such a miracle in itself that the child that has been growing inside you for months is now cuddled in your arms. There are the hopes and dreams for the future. You see part of yourself in this little helpless human being, and there is unbelievable joy in the process. But that's just when everything goes the way it is supposed to, right? What happens when basically everything falls apart?

That's where faith comes in.

If you don't believe in God, these concepts will be far more difficult for you to grasp than someone who does believe in God, or at least some form of higher power. I pray that God will reveal himself through my words and that he can indeed become real to you. Because, my friend, if you do not have him with you, and you are facing a mountain of fear and doubt I can truthfully say I don't know how you are going to make it through. The good news is, I can tell you without question that, with God and his powerful grace, you can and will endure whatever is set before you.

Believe it or not, I am encouraged by the thought that God always has a purpose for the storms in our lives. What I have come to realize in the last year and a half is that we are faced with storms as a way for God to get us beyond ourselves and dependent on him. The storms don't necessarily mean that I have done something wrong and this is now my punishment. I did, however, go through a stage in my grief when that was exactly what I thought, but I have come to understand that it doesn't matter how many times I messed up in the past, Karson's death was not God's way of punishing me for all the bad things I had done. Instead, I think God sends the storms not to sink our ships but rather to settle our souls—to prove to us again and again that he is in control of every aspect of our lives.

Some might wonder why, if I had such strong faith in God and trusted him to heal Karson, why didn't he do it? Wouldn't it have been a more powerful miracle if after all the diagnosis and her not breathing that she would turn out to be just fine and alive and well with us right now? My answer to that is that she came long enough to show each of us what pure unconditional love can do in this world. She lived her purpose to the full then went back home. James Dobson says in one of his books that when we wonder about God's timing, we must remind ourselves that none of us can look around the corner and see what lies ahead. Only God can see and comprehend all things in the future. When we put our trust in an all-knowing God to act in our best interest at all times, we can have hope.

"Consider it pure joy, my brothers, whenever you face trials of many kinds, because you know that the testing of your faith develops perseverance" (James 1:2–3). I truly think it is that simple. Every one of us was created for a purpose. Some of us fulfill that purpose in a short time, some it takes forty or fifty years, and some live to great old age still fulfilling their purpose. Only God knows the number of our days and what that purpose is. Some of us may figure it out as we go along, and others might not be realized until in death we meet our Savior for all the unanswered questions.

I have been known to tell people that my odds aren't very good. Actually, the opposite may be true. The odds were one in five thousand that Karson would have trisomy 13, and we hit that one on the head. After some genetic testing, we learned that it was even larger odds than that because neither Kevin nor I was a carrier of the disease. It was just a fluke. I should spend some serious time in Vegas if that is the case. Fortunately, I don't feel that way any longer either, and my statement has now changed to "the odds are great that God is doing something amazing in my life, and isn't it awesome that he wants to use Kevin, Karson, and my life as an example of his mighty love and power?" It wasn't a fluke. God knew what was going to happen from beginning to end.

There are many examples of this in the Bible as well. Take the story of Jesus walking on the water. The story in Mark 6:45–56 shows that he had a plan way before the disciples ever figured out what it was. He sent them out in the boat alone, insistent that they go without him. Do you think he knew there would be a storm? Of course he did. He also knew that he would walk on water in the midst of the storm and calm not only the wind and the waves but also their fears and doubts about who he was. He did the same in our lives. He walked on the overwhelming circumstances of Karson's disease and created a miracle before our very eyes, showing us all who he was. For more evidence of this, let's look back at the song that I claimed for our family days before we even knew that her diagnosis was death and months before Karson was actually born. The similarities amaze me.

In the song: A young child is brought to his mother and she holds him until he dies in her arms.

In our story: Karson wasn't breathing when she was born.

In the song: The woman runs straight to the man of God for his help.

In our story: I relied on God's strength throughout my pregnancy, and when Karson was born not breathing, I cried out to God in despair.

In the song: Elisha prays for the boy, and he breathes again.

In our story: God breathed new life into Karson twenty minutes after she was born.

In the song: God doesn't ever change; if you'll have that women's faith, he will send you a miracle.

In our story: We had our modern-day miracle that defied the odds, and we were able to say, "It is well."

You'll never get me to believe anything other than God gave me that song early on, taught my heart to trust him through the pain, and then he delivered just as he promised—our miracle. Karson went on to die just twelve days later, but by then all our prayers had been answered, and in God's divine wisdom, he called her home.

Answered Prayer

Believe it or not, there were a lot of answered prayers throughout Karson's journey. I prayed nightly that Karson would not die in my womb; she didn't. I wanted to hold her while she was alive; we had twelve glorious days with her. We wanted to take her home free from all the poking and prodding so we could remember her somewhere other than in the hospital; we had two wonderful days at home with her. We prayed for her complete healing; she received it on the thirteenth day. We asked God to be sure that one or both of us would be there when she died and that one of us would be holding her; we were both there, and she was in Kevin's arms. We prayed that she wouldn't struggle for life or suffer; there was no sign of struggle or fight to live. Finally, we asked that we would be able to find peace in our despair at the time of her death; we didn't question or fight it at the time—we just let her go.

Every single one of these prayers was answered, and it is indeed well within our souls. Yes, we miss our little girl, and selfishly, we would probably choose to have her back on this earth with us if we could. The truth is though, no matter how long we shared life with her on earth, it would have been too short. We've learned a lot about letting go and can accept that this was God's will, but we are not superhumans that don't wish it would've turned out differently.

Messages from the Other Side

Another thing that has really helped me get through my days of loneliness is to believe and embrace signs or messages from Karson. I cannot tell you the number of times that a particular song will come on at just the very instant I am thinking of her. You may say it is just coincidence, I choose to believe it is more than that. Someone once said that coincidence is only God's way of remaining anonymous. I believe in my heart those are moments God gives us to reassure us that our loved ones are okay. He understands our doubts and fears of the unknown, so he lets them send us little messages to get by until we can join them ourselves one day. I've had a number of dreams about Karson. I don't always remember them in detail; sometimes I just wake up knowing I had an encounter with her spirit because I feel happy at the thought of her and not sad.

One of my favorite stories happened to Kevin as he was on the road one day. One of the songs that touched both of us deeply is "The Streets of Heaven," by Sherrie Austin. One day, as Kevin was feeling pretty down and missing Karson even more than usual, he turned on his radio and "The Streets of Heaven" was playing. He listened, and as the song ended, he switched stations, and there it was again, and then yet again as he switched stations a third time—the song blared out at him. Kevin also longed for a dream about Karson and finally had one of his very own about a month ago. It is one he will never forget, no matter how silly it may seem. This is how he describes it:

He was sitting alone on a hill. All of a sudden, the OU marching band was there playing the Boomer Sooner fight song. I walked up holding Karson, and she had her eyes wide open and was laughing and clapping to the music. She was as happy as she could be. Kevin woke me up and told me he had just had the best dream about Karson and how wonderful it was to see her so happy. There was no sadness, and that is the picture that he gets to carry with him as he goes along.

I had an experience of my own about two months after Karson died. Some might call it a dream; others might say it was a message from beyond or even a visiting. I call it another miracle.

Kara and Kasi's Grandma Polly died a couple of months before Karson was born. Polly was an amazing woman of God with the faith of a saint. We talked a couple of times about the chance of Karson dying. Polly herself was on the verge of death after a long battle with cancer. Thankfully, she knew where her journey would end (or begin, as I would rather think of it). Anyhow, I asked her once that if they both got to heaven before I did, would she please watch out for Karson and take care of her. She assured me she would.

One night, after Karson had passed away, Kevin was on a trip and I was spending the night at Kara and Chad's. I always sleep in their extra bedroom located right off the kitchen. In my dream and in reality, I was doing just that. I have never had a dream like this before. It was so real. It was set up just like life really was. Usually dreams have some things that are farfetched or out of the ordinary in them. Not this time; it was exactly like it was in real life, down to the palm tree sheets on the bed.

In my dream, I had just gone to sleep when I heard a bunch of people in the front room of the house. I sat up so I could see what was going on. At the same time, the front screen door opened and in walked Polly. I could see her as plain as day, but it was obvious no one else could because they paid no attention to her. She looked beautiful and healthy. She was wearing a pretty pink blouse, and her hair looked like it had just been done at the salon. She walked straight toward me. As she is walking to me, I am thinking to myself, *Polly died, and she is in heaven.* When she reaches the bed, she sits down on the edge and says, "Hello, Lou." I'm trying my best to decipher what is going on, and then it dawns on me—if she is in heaven, then she has probably seen Karson. So I say, "Oh my gosh, have you seen

Karson?" She replies, "Yes, a few times, but truthfully, she is just so busy playing that we don't get much time to visit." I say, "Is she okay?" and Polly answers with a smile, "Karson is perfect." And then she was gone.

Struggles

This is excellent section to share with others!

I will admit those are the good times. Let me tell you that isn't how every day goes. Over the last nine months or so, Kevin and I have had our struggles. One of those struggles has been about our desire for another baby and when would it be okay to try again, or should we adopt and forgo the possibility of another sick child or miscarriage? I won't rehash all the discussions and disagreements but will just suffice it to say I was ready to do anything and everything to have another child as soon as possible and Kevin was not. Thankfully, God took both of our stubborn souls into account, and he, once again in his perfect timing, provided us with the answer when it was right.

I heard a wonderful pastor named Britt Merrick from Carpentria, California, speak one Sunday morning about the storms in our lives, and in his wisdom, he said this, "If you are waiting on God for something in your life, it is because he is working in you something for eternal glory." It doesn't mean he isn't listening and that he isn't going to give you an answer; it simply means you're not ready yet for what is to come.

"Therefore we do not lose heart. Though outwardly we are wasting away, yet inwardly we are being renewed day by day. For our light and momentary troubles are achieving for us an eternal glory that far outweighs them all. So we fix our eyes not on what is seen, but on what is unseen. For what is seen is temporary, but what is unseen is eternal" (2 Corinthians 4:16–18)

There's that concept of faith again. Ever get the feeling God is trying to teach us something? I assure you it is a lesson I still have not gotten completely comfortable with. I still want things in my time. I want God to get on the same page with me rather than vice versa. I think I know what is best for me. It is a constant struggle for me to embrace his will in my life. That is why when this past April I found out I was pregnant again, I was unable to claim that joy for my life. I was petrified with fear. I was so afraid that something was going to go wrong, that he would again test my faith by allowing me to go through yet another loss. I have had bad dreams, panic attacks, mood swings, and depression over this baby. Not until about a week ago did I feel better. I was able to meet with Dr. Stanley, the same specialist we saw with Karson, and with his medical expertise, he was able to tell me that this baby girl is healthy, with no evidence of any problems.

After everything that God has brought us through, I still doubted him. Instead of expecting goodness from God, I feared the worst. I had to wait to hear it from human voices before I allowed some relief to come over me. This proves to me that faith is a never-ending process. My dad says God doesn't care how many times we have to learn the lessons; the important thing is that we realize God is in the journey, no matter how many times we have to make it.

"Wait for the Lord; be strong and take heart and wait for the Lord" (Psalm 27:14).

Moving On

One thing that Kevin and I have determined not to do is let another child, particularly this baby girl I am now carrying, to take the place of Karson. We both hope for some similarities, but I never want to find myself placing what I think would've been Karson's characteristics on Konner, and in turn, I don't want to ever let go of the fact that Karson is a member of this family. She will always be my first-born, the one who gave me the gift of being a mother for the first time. I know specifics about her will get harder and harder to recall; that is the other reason for this book. I want our other children to know about their big sister. I want them to know how strong she was and to know that they will meet her in heaven one day. I don't want to build a shrine to her; I just want there to be an awareness and a knowledge that even though not physically here, she is a part of our lives forever.

I mentioned earlier that after the first day of leaving Karson's urn at home, I wouldn't do that again. So far, that remains true, and I don't foresee it changing any time in the future. It's one of those things that work for us. One of the comforts we allow ourselves to indulge in. The little lamb is all we physically have left of Karson. To take her with us somehow keeps her more real to us. We talk to her, fuss over her, take turns keeping her, and I even buy different scarves to tie around her neck for the different seasons. I've learned not to be afraid of let my feelings out or to let what others might think detour me from doing something out of the ordinary.

There are many different stages and ways to handle grief, and everyone's timetable is different. What's important to remember is all the stages and differences are okay. God deals with each of us differently, and no single way of expressing grief is better than another. It is simply how you handle grief. No one can tell you the best way to respond to the loss of a loved one or how long it will take you to mourn. It is an individualized process you take with God.

Where in the world Is Karson?

As I said, I don't want to be overbearing with Karson to our other kids, so I have decided to make life with her some sort of game. Kevin and I have already started playing it. It is called "Where in the World Is Karson?" Kind of like "Where in the World Is Waldo?" We take Karson on all our trips with us. Whether it is to the mountains of Colorado or the beaches of Mexico, she goes where we go. In each of the places, we take pictures of Karson for her "Where in the World Is Karson?" photo album. I think it is a fun, non-scary way for us to incorporate her into our lives for years to come. I also think she will be a learning tool for us to use to teach our kids about death and about the joy and promise of heaven. It is the right answer for us at this time in our lives, and we believe God knew what would work for us, and he helped us choose the lamb urn the day we took her to the funeral home.

Realizing the Blessings of God in Your Life

As I close with a few last thoughts, I hope that my ramblings and writings in some way helped you or touched a special place in your heart. If it can do half of what it has done for me to write it, then I know you have been blessed. I want to end by encouraging you to seek God in the good and the bad. I promise he is there in both. Remember that the storms we encounter in our lives have the potential to not only end up blessing us but also those around us. You never know what God has in store for you or the lives that you may change because of a storm you have endured. That's the awesomeness of our God.

When things are good in our lives, we often lose sight of God, but He never seems more faithful than in the rough times. Trust him in both. Trust him with your life, with that of your spouse and children, and even your unborn children. Give him reign to work; don't tighten the noose around his neck and tell him when and where he should do something miraculous. If we leave the power of life and death in his hands instead of taking it upon ourselves, we can rest assured that his most good and perfect will will be done. I said earlier that I have a lot of questions for God someday. I don't really believe that when I get to heaven, God and I will sit down and go over my list of questions. What I really think will happen is that as soon as I enter the presence of the Lord, I will no longer have any questions. Either they will be answered within my heart, or they simply will no longer matter compared to the splendor of heaven. As Dobson says,

"One glimpse of him will be all that we shall need for the rest of eternity concerning the mysteries of life."

I want to assure you that every day begins and ends with his purpose. There isn't one single detail that escapes his eye. There isn't one trial that doesn't touch him, and nothing is beyond his compassion. Don't get so lost in yourself that you miss the miracles God is sending your way, even in times of trouble. Recognize his hand at work, and accept his many blessings in your life. And most of all, when you get down, I encourage you to think of heaven and how our journeys will all one day come to perfect completion when we see our Lord face-to-face.

Here She Comes

One of my favorite things to do is to conjure up thoughts of what Karson must be doing in heaven and all the fun she must be having. I don't know why, but I picture her as a little two- or three-year-old instead of as a baby. Maybe because as a baby, she wouldn't be running and playing, and that is definitely what I think she is doing in heaven. I think she is having the time of her life, living every moment with a smile on her face, all in the glory and presence of Jesus. I still think of her in the little dress she had on when she died, the one with all the butterflies on it, and I picture her with butterfly wings of her own. I see her little bare feet running and jumping and praising Jesus.

There is a poem by Henry Van Dyke that says it all for me. I'll share the poem and then explain why it gives me such joy and comfort.

> I am standing upon the seashore. A ship at my side spreads her white sails to the morning breeze and starts for the blue ocean. She is an object of beauty and strength. I stand and watch her until at length she hangs like a speck of white cloud just where the sea and sky come to mingle with each other.
>
> Then someone at my side says, "There, she is gone." "Gone where?"
>
> Gone from my sight. That is all. She is just as large in mast and hull and spar as she was when

she left my side and she is just as able to bear her load of living freight to her destined port. Her diminished size is in me, not in her. And just at the moment when someone at my side says, "There, she is gone," there are voices ready to take up the glad shout—"Here she comes!" And that is dying.

And that is exactly how I picture it happened. That morning when God sent the angels to get Karson, I think in that very moment we knew she was gone, on the other side in glory land, Jesus had all the other children of heaven waiting to greet Karson when she arrived. As she entered the pearly gates, they were jumping up and down saying, "Here she comes, here comes Karson!" And then they enveloped her into their little clan, and off they went to explore and show her the wonders of heaven.

She is able to bask in the beauty of God endlessly. She doesn't hurt or scream out because she is in pain. The only sounds from her are squeals of delight. That's how I want to picture my little girl forever, and I look forward to the day when it is me the angels are escorting to heaven, and there I will again see my daughter, now the leader of the pack, jumping up and down saying, "Here she comes, here comes my mom!"

And that is heaven.

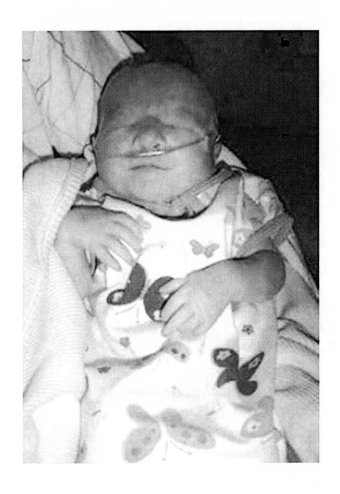

About the Author

Lou Bickerstaff lives in Ada, Oklahoma, with her husband, Kevin, and two school-age daughters, Konner and Kennadee. She enjoys spending time with her husband watching their daughters play soccer, basketball, and rodeo. She is also stepmom to two grown daughters and Mimi to four grandsons. Beach vacationing, snow-skiing, reading, and spending time with family and friends at their ranch are among her favorite activities.

After working several years in public relations and marketing and then being a stay-at-home mom, she went back to school for her nursing degree and is now a registered nurse working in labor and delivery. Lou attributes her experience with Karson as what ignited the desire in her heart for nursing. She believes it is her chance to carry on Karson's legacy by sharing Jesus's love with people going through similar situations and losses.